CLASSIC
LOCOMOTIVES

STEAM AND DEISEL POWER IN 700 PHOTOGRAPHS

BRIAN SOLOMON

Voyageur Press

First published in 2009, 2010, and 2011 by Voyageur Press, an imprint of MBI Publishing Company, 400 First Avenue North, Suite 400, Minneapolis, MN 55401 USA

Voyageur Press titles are also available at discounts in bulk quantity for industrial or sales-promotional use. For details write to Special Sales Manager at MBI Publishing Company, 400 First Avenue North, Suite 400, Minneapolis, MN 55401 USA.

Library of Congress Cataloging-in-Publication Data
Solomon, Brian, 1966–
   Classic locomotives : steam and diesel power in 700 photographs / Brian Solomon.
       p. cm.
   Summary: "The collection of three previously published volumes presents the history of locomotives from early steam power through today's massive diesel-electric models. Illustrated with 700 photographs accompanied by in-depth, informative captions" –Provided by publisher.
   "First published in 2009, 2010, and 2011 by Voyageur Press, an imprint of MBI Publishing Company" – T.p. verso.
   Includes index.
   ISBN 978-0-7603-4528-3 (softcover)
   1. Steam locomotives–History. 2. Diesel locomotives–History. 3. Electro-diesel locomotives–History. I. Title.
   TJ603.S668 2013
   625.260973--dc23
                                       2013009223

Cover photo: Popular with railroad enthusiasts, Southern Pacific No. 2472 is a Class P-8 Pacific type built by Baldwin in 1921. It's seen here in Sacramento in 1991. *Brian Solomon*
Spine: Pennylvania Railroad RF-16 No. 9595 rests at Kinsman Yard in Cleveland, Ohio, on July 11, 1958. *Richard J. Solomon*
Frontispiece: Former Central Vermont No. 3604, owned by Genesee Valley Transportation, is seen at Rochester & Southern's Brooks Avenue Yard in Rochester, New York. *Brian Solomon*
Title pages: A Metra MP36PH-3S leads a commuter train at Grayslake, Illinois, in December 2004. *Chris Guss*
Back cover, left: In June 1961, pristine Canadian National FP9 and a B-unit catch the sun at Burk's Falls, Ontario, with train No. 41 running from Toronto to North Bay. *Richard J. Solomon*
Back cover, middle: Since 1962, No. 3 has served as a tourist locomotive at the Roaring Camp & Big Trees at Felton, California, where it brings visitors over a re-created narrow-gauge logging railroad. *Brian Solomon*
Back cover, right: BNSF No. 5973 departs U.S. Steel's Minntac plant in Mt. Iron, Minnesota, beginning its all-rail trip south to the steelmaker's facility near Birmingham, Alabama. *Todd Mavec*

To find out more about our books, visit us online at www.voyageurpress.com.

Editor: Dennis Pernu
Design Manager: James Kegley
Designer: Jennie Tischler

Printed in China

Contents

Steam Power

Introduction

Introduction

The locomotive was one of the foremost products of the Industrial Revolution. The steam locomotive had evolved in Britain from stationary industrial engines. Richard Trevithick demonstrated his pioneer locomotive at the Pen-y-Darran Iron Works in Wales on February 13, 1804. Over the next two decades, various small locomotives were built for operation on short industrial tramways. George Stephenson's Stockton & Darlington Railway opened in 1821. Considered the first public railway, it used locomotives to haul freight and passengers, establishing a pattern of operation rapidly copied across Britain and exported to the United States.

Equally influential was Stephenson's Liverpool & Manchester Railway (L&M), opened in 1829. To forward locomotive design, the L&M held a locomotive competition. The winning machine was the *Rocket*, built by Stephenson's son Robert. Its overwhelming success was due to its use of three basic locomotive design principles: a multi-tubular (fire tube) boiler, forced draft from exhaust steam, and direct linkage between the piston and drive wheels. This prototype established the foundation for most subsequent successful steam locomotive designs, not just in Britain, but around the world.

America was only a few years behind Britain in adopting the steam railway. In the 1820s, American engineers traveled across the Atlantic to study and import the new technology. In 1827, the Delaware & Hudson Canal Company planned a coal tramway from the mines near Carbondale, Pennsylvania, to its canal head at Honesdale. The D&H's Horatio Allen traveled to Britain and imported both rails and four complete locomotives for use on this primordial American line. At least one of the locomotives was fired up, but it proved an inauspicious beginning for steam in America, as these locomotives were deemed too heavy for regular operation and never performed as intended.

Within a few years, other railroads were underway. Some followed D&H's lead and imported British locomotives; others bought locomotives built locally. While some American locomotives used homegrown designs, the vast majority were technological descendants of Stephenson's Rocket. By the mid-1830s, several locomotive manufacturers had been established in the United States. The most significant, and ultimately the largest, was Philadelphia's Baldwin Locomotive Works.

American locomotives needed to fulfill different requirements than their British counterparts and followed a different evolutionary path. Often using tracks constructed to lower standards than in Britain, American locomotives required leading guide wheels and substantial pilots to keep from derailing. Also, American railroads looked to achieve ever greater levels of operating efficiency, and most didn't suffer from the variety of operating constraints that limited boiler size in Britain. In the twentieth century, locomotive size and output were pushed to the limit. Ultimately, American railroads operated some of the largest, heaviest, and most powerful steam locomotives ever built.

The desire for greater efficiency led American railroads to abandon steam, first on a small scale in favor of electric motive power, and then on a wide scale in favor of diesel-electric locomotives. Following World War II, diesels were ready for mass production and railroads began the expensive conversion to diesel operations. The last commercial steam locomotives were delivered in the late 1940s, and a small number of railroads resisted the conversion to diesel for a few years. Most notably, the Norfolk & Western (N&W) continued to build its own steam locomotives until the early 1950s. Nationally, by the mid-1950s, the once ubiquitous steam locomotive was becoming increasingly rare. Even the N&W recognized the superior economics of the diesel-electric, and in 1960 concluded its revenue main-line steam operations. The steam era was over, although isolated pockets of steam survived on a handful of short lines for a few more years.

The switch to diesel power occurred at the same time the railroads were losing their transport supremacy. Although freight remained important in many areas, the rapid decline of intercity passenger services after World War II changed public perception of the railroad. By the 1960s, there emerged nostalgia for steam locomotives. Some railroads had set aside steam locomotives for preservation. Other locomotives were acquired by individuals, museums, and communities for display and a few for operation. Of the estimated 138,000 steam locomotives built for U.S. railways, approximately 1,900 escaped scrapping. The majority of these are relatively small switchers and light freight locomotives built in the first decades of the twentieth century. Sadly, relatively few of the earliest machines survived and only select examples of the largest, fastest, and most impressive locomotives of the late steam era were preserved.

Over the years, a small number of preserved locomotives have been restored to operating condition for excursion services. Typically, these units are operated seasonally by railway museums or tourist railways. A few large locomotives have been restored for main-line trips. Although steam locomotives are comparatively simple machines, it is an extremely expensive proposition to maintain one in operating condition. Locomotives require periodic overhauls of the boiler, firebox, and other key components. Most surviving steam

Previous pages:
Consolidation No. 40 left Pennsylvania's Baldwin Locomotive Works in November 1925 for South Carolina's Lancaster & Chester Railroad. Today, it's much closer to its birthplace on the New Hope & Ivyland, a meandering 17-mile-long short line connecting its namesake towns in southeastern Pennsylvania. On a damp June afternoon, No. 40 storms up the grade out of New Hope. *Brian Solomon*

locomotives are at least 70 years old (many are much older) and occasionally develop problems that are costly to correct.

Today, the roster of working steam is like a big game of musical chairs. A locomotive that has worked for decades may be withdrawn from service and placed on static display. Other locomotives, cold since diesels made them redundant, may be returned to service. Some steam locomotives have regularly worked for years; others have made only occasional appearances. Of the many machines featured in this book, most have seen service since the end of revenue steam, although some are no longer in service as of this writing. These locomotives may operate again, provided there are sufficient interest, finances, and know-how to put them back into action.

The last chapter of this book focuses on steam power overseas, especially in Britain. Not only did the locomotive originate in Britain, but Britain has the most intensive and comprehensive railway preservation culture in the world. There, dozens of historic railways operate beautifully restored steam locomotives to the thrill of the public.

Steam was through on most American railways by the early to mid-1950s. By the early 1960s, a groundswell of railway enthusiasm brought steam back for excursion services. Where a steam locomotive wouldn't have earned a passing glance from the public a generation earlier, it was now a nostalgic attraction. In July 1966, enthusiasts scramble for the best angle of Burlington No. 4960 at Walnut, Illinois. *John Gruber*

Whyte Classification System

The most common American method of classifying steam locomotives is the Whyte system. Locomotive types are described by the arrangement of leading, driving, and trailing wheels. A zero indicates absence of wheels in one of these locations. For example, the classic American type, which has four leading wheels, four driving wheels, and no trailing wheels, is designated a 4-4-0. The Atlantic type has four leading wheels, four driving wheels, and two trailing wheels and is designated 4-4-2. Locomotives such as Mallets and Duplexes, which have more than one set of drivers and running gear, count each grouping of driving wheels. The Union Pacific Big Boy is so classified as a 4-8-8-4. Locomotives with built-in tanks rather than tenders have a letter "T" following the wheel count (for example, 0-6-0T).

The standard wheel arrangements have names associated with them. Early names were descriptive, such as the 4-6-0 Ten-Wheeler, but later names tended to represent the railroad that first used the arrangement. The 4-8-4, generally known as a Northern type after the Northern Pacific, is also known by a host of other names.

Wheel Arrangement	Whyte Classification	Name
<OOO	0-6-0	—
<ooOO	4-4-0	American
<ooOOo	4-4-2	Atlantic
<oOOO	2-6-0	Mogul
<oOOOo	2-6-2	Prairie
<ooOOO	4-6-0	Ten-Wheeler
<ooOOOo	4-6-2	Pacific
<ooOOOoo	4-6-4	Hudson
<oOOOO	2-8-0	Consolidation
<oOOOOo	2-8-2	Mikado
<oOOOOoo	2-8-4	Berkshire
<ooOOOO	4-8-0	Twelve-Wheeler
<ooOOOOo	4-8-2	Mountain
<ooOOOOoo	4-8-4	Northern
<oOOOOO	2-10-0	Decapod
<oOOOOOo	2-10-2	Santa Fe
<oOOOOOoo	2-10-4	Texas
<ooOOOOOOo	4-12-2	Union Pacific
<ooOOO OOOoo	4-6-6-4	Challenger
<ooOOOO OOOOoo	4-8-8-4	Big Boy

Chapter 1
Building Eastern Industry

Building Eastern Industry

The first North American railways were built in the East. These railways served established cities and towns, and were instrumental in the emergence of the eastern industrial manufacturing economy. Railroad companies competed for territory, often building parallel and overlapping infrastructure to reach the most lucrative sources of traffic, resulting in by far the most intensive railway network on the continent. Lines tapped coal and iron mines, timber stands, limestone quarries, and dozens of other resources. Intensive commuter services were developed around Boston, New York, and Philadelphia. Long-distance passenger trains connected virtually every community in the East. The busiest railroads required four-track main lines to accommodate the high volume of freight and passenger traffic. Secondary routes and branch lines were built to virtually every town of significant size, while trunk lines reached from eastern cities to gateways in the Midwest.

As the railroad network expanded and companies vied for traffic and territory, locomotive design progressed. Ever larger, faster, more powerful, and, ultimately, more efficient machines were built. In the nineteenth century, dozens of manufacturers built locomotives commercially. The largest manufacturers were Baldwin Locomotive Works in Philadelphia, Pennsylvania, established in 1831; the Schenectady Locomotive Works in Schenectady, New York, established in 1848; and Brooks Locomotive Works in Dunkirk, New York, established in 1869. Baldwin emerged as the largest builder, and in 1901, to counter Baldwin, several smaller locomotive builders, including Schenectady and Brooks, joined forces to form the American Locomotive Company, commonly known as "Alco." The same year, the Lima Locomotive and Machine Company of Lima, Ohio—which had built the geared Shay type since 1880— was reorganized as the Lima Locomotive Works to build conventional locomotives. In the first half of the twentieth century, Baldwin, Alco, and Lima were the most significant commercial builders in the United States. Several eastern railroads—notably, the Pennsylvania and the Norfolk & Western— also designed and constructed large numbers of their own locomotives. Several significant builders of smaller industrial and switching locomotives were also located in the East, including the Climax Manufacturing Company in Corry, Pennsylvania; Vulcan Iron Works in Wilkes-Barre, Pennsylvania; and H. K. Porter Company of Pittsburgh.

Various railroads, preservation groups, historical societies, and private organizations have made main-line steam trips a reality in the East, enabling some of the largest preserved locomotives to work the main lines again. The Reading Company operated its T-1 4-8-4s on Reading Rambles beginning in the late 1950s. Starting in the 1960s, the Southern Railway organized trips on its lines, and both the Southern and its successor, Norfolk Southern (NS), have operated locomotives on trips over its lines, including the Norfolk & Western's famous J-class No. 611 and A-class No. 1218. Although, the NS's steam program concluded in 1994, operation of the engines allowed thousands of people to experience big steam decades after revenue operations had ended.

In the 1980s, the famous Pennsylvania Railroad Class K4s Pacific No. 1361 was removed from its perch at the Horseshoe Curve, restored to operating condition, and briefly resurrected. Elsewhere, the Chesapeake & Ohio's massive 4-8-4 No. 614 has made many outings, while railroads such as the New York, Susquehanna & Western and the Reading & Northern have operated steam trips over their lines.

Main-line steam trips, however, have been relatively rare occurrences in the East. The best place to experience steam is at one of the many tourist railways or railroad museums that focus on steam preservation. In New England, the Conway Scenic Railway in New Hampshire and the Valley Railroad in Connecticut have regularly operated steam for several decades. The state of Pennsylvania hosts some of America's finest historic lines and museums, including the Strasburg Rail Road and the Railroad Museum of Pennsylvania at Strasburg; the Steamtown National Historic Site in Scranton; the East Broad Top Railroad at Orbisonia; and the Wanamaker, Kempton & Southern at Kempton, among others. Farther south, in Maryland, the Baltimore & Ohio Railroad Museum and the Western Maryland Scenic Railroad are worth the trip.

Previous pages:
Southern Railway No. 4501 works between St. Matthews and Branchville, South Carolina, on September 4, 1970. This handsome Mikado was so popular that it was the sole topic of a book by late *Trains* magazine editor David P. Morgan. *George W. Kowanski*

The first American-built steam locomotive made its public debut on August 28, 1830. Constructed by New York industrialist Peter Cooper to demonstrate to the Baltimore & Ohio the ability of American industry to produce working locomotives, this machine successfully hauled 13 tons at 4 miles per hour. *Brian Solomon*

Left: Unlike most railroad locomotives, Peter Cooper's employed a vertical boiler derived from marine practice. Because of its small size, this curious machine was compared with a popular circus figure named Tom Thumb, and the name stuck. The B&O's 1927 replica weighs roughly 7 tons compared with Cooper's original, estimated to weigh only 1 ton. *Brian Solomon*

Above: In the formative days of American railroading, Peter Cooper's locomotive led to a distinctive design first built by Phineas Davis and later by Ross Winans. Ultimately, this design died out in favor of more successful designs based on Robert Stephenson's famous *Rocket.* On November 9, 1996, B&O successor CSX borrowed the 1927-built replica for show on the original B&O main line at Ellicott City, Maryland. *Brian Solomon*

Above: Horatio Allen, one of America's railroad pioneers, earned a reputation on Pennsylvania's Delaware & Hudson in the 1820s. He made history by importing British-made locomotives to work the line. Although unsuccessful in that effort, he soon moved to the South Carolina Railroad, where he ordered a pioneering American-designed locomotive called the *Best Friend of Charleston. George W. Kowanski*

Opposite top: South Carolina Railroad's *Best Friend of Charleston* was designed by E. L. Miller of Charleston and constructed at the West Point Foundry in New York City. It was delivered in autumn 1830. In June 1831, *Best Friend* was destroyed by a boiler explosion. This 1928-built replica was posed with Southern Railway No. 722 at Charleston in 1970 to mark the South Carolina Railroad's 140th anniversary. *George W. Kowanski*

Opposite bottom: On January 15, 1831, *Best Friend* became the first American locomotive to haul a regularly scheduled passenger train. The replica is owned by the city of Charleston. As of 2008, the locomotive was on loan to South Carolina Railroad successor Norfolk Southern and displayed at the company's offices in Atlanta, Georgia. *George W. Kowanski*

The Norfolk & Western is remembered for retaining big steam power longer than any other major railroad in the United States. Its late-era designs were among the finest steam locomotives to work American rails. N&W's Roanoke Shops turned out 14 well-crafted J-class 4-8-4s that set performance and reliability records. In one test run, a J reached 110 miles per hour with a 15-car 1,025-ton train. In service, the 4-8-4s turned 15,000 miles per month. *Brian Solomon*

Above: Long ago eclipsed by its famous sister, Norfolk & Western J No. 610 is serviced at Schafer's Crossing in Roanoke, Virginia, on July 31, 1958. N&W's sleek, modern, J-class locomotives were routinely assigned to the railroad's finest long-distance passenger runs, including the *Pocahontas* and the *Powhatan Arrow*. *Richard Jay Solomon*

Left: In the 1980s, the Norfolk & Western restored No. 611 to active service, and it became a regular star of steam excursions. In August 1994, No. 611 races toward the setting sun west of Valparaiso, Indiana, on one of its final excursion runs for Norfolk Southern. After more than a decade of excursions, the streamliner was returned to the Virginia Museum of Transportation at Roanoke. Its boiler has been cold ever since. *Brian Solomon*

Retired in 1959, N&W No. 611 was preserved at the Virginia Museum of Transportation, making it one of only a handful of streamlined steam locomotives to escape scrapping. In 1982, Norfolk Southern restored No. 611 to service, and for the next dozen years it operated numerous excursions across the NS system. Here, it works westward at Eggleston, Virginia. *George W. Kowanski*

Left: Along with J-class No. 611, another star of Norfolk Southern's steam program was A-class No. 1218. On August 1, 1987, NS choreographed operation of these two locomotives on its former N&W main line west of Roanoke at Christiansburg, Virginia. *George W. Kowanski*

Above: Bathed in its own smoke and steam, N&W No. 611 charges west at Hardy, West Virginia, on October 23, 1982. In their day, the N&W's J-class locomotives were noted as exceptionally smooth-running machines. Precision counterbalancing helped minimize destructive dynamic forces. *George W. Kowanski*

The star of Western Maryland Scenic's popular excursion service is No. 734, a locomotive typical of the large-boiler 2-8-0 Consolidation types once common in freight service in the United States. *Brian Solomon*

Left: Western Maryland Scenic Railroad operates the old Western Maryland Railroad grade west of Cumberland, Maryland, to Frostburg. Here, No. 734 works upgrade at Helmstetter's Curve. *Brian Solomon*

Above: No. 734 was built by Alco and labored in ore service on the Lake Superior & Ishpeming in Michigan's Upper Peninsula. Today, it is dressed as a Western Maryland locomotive for excursion service. *Brian Solomon*

The Southern Railway concluded regular steam operations in 1953, but No. 4501 wasn't among the last steam to work in revenue service on the Southern. It had been sold to the Kentucky & Tennessee Railway back in 1948. In 1964, the Tennessee Valley Railroad Museum restored the old Mikado, and in 1966 it began working main-line excursions on old home rails. Here, No. 4501 is surrounded by adoring fans at Salisbury, North Carolina, on August 25, 1966. *John Gruber*

Above: Baldwin built Southern No. 4501 in 1911. The Southern's Ms-class ("s" for "superheating") Mikados were handsome, nicely proportioned, and powerful locomotives but otherwise unremarkable in their day. The Southern revived No. 4501 and made it a star of its steam program, where it entertained tens of thousands of people in two decades of main-line excursions. Working the Seaboard Coast Line rails in 1970, No. 4501 heads southward at Yemassee, South Carolina. *George W. Kowanski*

Left: On September 4, 1970, Southern Railway No. 4501, with a National Railway Historical Society–sponsored excursion from Washington, D.C., to Charleston, South Carolina, pauses at Columbia. On the locomotive's pilot is the Southern's president, W. Graham Claytor, who was instrumental in putting the locomotive in main-line excursion service. In 1982, Ronald Reagan appointed Claytor to run Amtrak. *George W. Kowanski*

Right: After the Reading's regular steam operations were discontinued, it assigned three of its Class T-1 4-8-4s to "Reading Ramble" excursion service on lines in eastern Pennsylvania. Nos. 2100 and 2102 lead an excursion in October 1964. *Richard Jay Solomon*

Above: Working west on the Central Railroad of New Jersey, Reading No. 2102 passes Netherwood, New Jersey, in 1972. A popular excursion locomotive for decades, No. 2102 has resided in recent years on the Blue Mountain & Reading/Reading & Northern, which operates former Reading Company routes in Pennsylvania. *George W. Kowanski*

During 1945 and 1947, when most lines were ordering new diesels, the Reading Company constructed 30 4-8-4s using boiler components from retired 2-8-0 Consolidations. No. 2102 was photographed in February 1972 at Hampton, New Jersey, while on an excursion over the Central Railroad of New Jersey from Elizabeth, New Jersey, to Bethlehem, Pennsylvania. *George W. Kowanski*

Right: On a locomotive, the valve gear serves a function similar to that of a transmission on an automobile. Consisting of rods, eccentrics, and links, the valve gear allows the engineer to control the position of the valves that direct the flow of the steam to the cylinders, thus adjusting the power and direction of the engine. Baker valve gear, seen here on C&O No. 614, was one of several patented arrangements used on select late-era steam locomotives. *Brian Solomon*

Above: An excursion train led by Chesapeake & Ohio Greenbrier No. 614 rolls eastward across Moodna Viaduct at Salisbury Mills, on its way from Port Jervis, New York, to Hoboken, New Jersey. This massive former–Erie Railroad viaduct takes its name from Moodna Creek, which runs through the valley. *Brian Solomon*

Chesapeake & Ohio No. 614 works east on the former Erie main line at S curves near Tuxedo, New York. This magnificent machine was one of five that Lima built for the coal-hauling C&O in 1948. On the C&O, 4-8-4s were known as Greenbriers, named for the Greenbrier River. Where some railroads ordered 4-8-4s for freight, the C&O's were designed for heavy passenger service. *Brian Solomon*

The C&O continued buying new steam locomotives after World War II, when most lines were buying only diesels. C&O J-3a No. 614 charges through Tuxedo, New York, with more than 20 passenger cars in tow in June 1997. *Brian Solomon*

Above: By 1948, few railroads were ordering new steam, which made the C&O's Greenbriers something of a novelty in postwar motive power and among the last 4-8-4s built in the United States. In September 1980, C&O No. 614 ascends Baltimore & Ohio's famous 17-Mile Grade at Bond, Maryland. *George W. Kowanski*

Left: The C&O's final Greenbriers were considered very modern, featuring roller bearings on all axles and side rods, aluminum cabs and boiler jacketing, and other late-era equipment and accessories. *Brian Solomon*

Right: Typically, Lima builder's plates were diamond shaped, while Baldwin's were circular and Alco's rectangular. This difference made it relatively easy to tell the builder of big steam without the need to study the fine print. *Brian Solomon*

Above: Chesapeake & Ohio No. 614 was one powerful set of wheels. With 72-inch wheels and 27 1/2×30-inch cylinders, and operating with 255 psi boiler pressure, this machine could get up and go. In June 1997, No. 614 makes a show of it at Port Jervis, New York. *Brian Solomon*

A low headlight and a high bell were typical of most C&O late-era steam power. Mechanically, the C&O's J-3a 4-8-4s were near cousins to the Nickel Plate Road's S-class Berkshires. Working an excursion train on the former Erie Graham Line, No. 614 pounds the rails near Salisbury Mills, New York. *Brian Solomon*

Right: The stainless-steel trim, headlight, and number board on Chesapeake & Ohio Class L-1 4-6-4 No. 490 typified the popular art deco styling of the period. The reign of the C&O's streamlined Hudson was pretty short, ending when the railroad bought Electro-Motive E-units in 1951. *Brian Solomon*

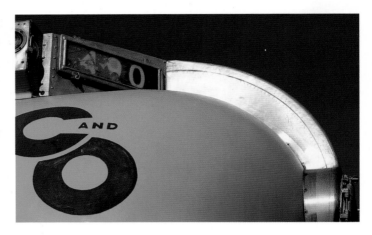

Above: C&O No. 490 works the main line in Kentucky on July 2, 1947. Today, this is one of only a few preserved Hudson types in the United States. *J. R. Quinn collection*

Early locomotive streamlining was intended to reduce wind resistance and thus improve fuel consumption. Later attempts were largely to make locomotives seem modern. *Brian Solomon*

Above: No. 65 has been a popular attraction since the Wanamaker, Kempton & Southern acquired it from Safe Harbor Water Power Corporation in 1970. This handsome saddle-tank type is characteristic of small industrial switch engines found all across North America. Here, it captures the essence of rural railroading while working up a short grade south of Wanamaker, Pennsylvania, on a former Reading Company branch line. *Brian Solomon*

Right: Steam railroading at night is a visceral experience: the distractions of daytime are subdued, accentuating the machine's sounds and aromas, and allowing its power to resonate in the soul. Wanamaker, Kempton & Southern No. 65 is bathed in its own steam at the Kempton, Pennsylvania, station after finishing its "Harvest Moon" special run to Wanamaker. *Brian Solomon*

No. 65 was a 0-6-0T built by H. K. Porter Company of Pittsburgh and sold in 1930 to the Safe Harbor Water Power Corporation, which used it in construction of the Safe Harbor dam along the Susquehanna River. Unlike larger locomotive manufacturers such as Baldwin and Alco that built customized designs to meet individual railroad specifications, Porter specialized in manufacturing stock-designed, small- to moderate-sized industrial locomotives. *Brian Solomon*

Pioneer Tunnel Coal Mine No. 1 is maintained to haul short excursions on this industrial railway at Ashland, Pennsylvania. On a humid summer morning, crewmembers douse hot cinders dumped from the firebox. Vulcan Iron Works was one of several locomotive builders in Pennsylvania. Vulcan built more than 4,000 locomotives between 1874 and 1950, focusing its production on small industrial types such as this 0-4-0T. *Brian Solomon*

Above: The Pioneer Colliery was opened in 1853 and closed in 1931. After 1873, the mine was part of the Reading Company empire. The line was rebuilt as a tourist attraction that provides views of the Mahanoy Mountains and old open-pit coal mines. Tracks are narrow compared with the main line—just 42 inches between the flanges. Pioneer Tunnel Coal Mine locomotive No. 1 is named after politician Henry Clay. *Brian Solomon*

Left: Instead of more modern piston valves, Pioneer Tunnel Coal Mine locomotive No. 1 uses traditional slide valves, easily identified by the boxy appendage above the cylinder. Small cylinders and tiny drive wheels are sufficient for moving coal jennies from the mine. *Brian Solomon*

Above: Middletown & Hummelstown is a Pennsylvania short line operating a few miles of former Reading Company trackage. It runs seasonal passenger excursions using diesels and this well-preserved former Canadian National 2-6-0. Locomotives with six-coupled driving wheels and a leading, pivoting two-wheeled pony truck came on the North American scene about 1860. Compared with the tiny 4-4-0 locomotives of the period, the 2-6-0 arrangement seemed enormous and so these locomotives were called Moguls. *Brian Solomon*

Right: The M&H's former Canadian National 2-6-0 Mogul type is a nicely balanced machine akin to No. 89, which works nearby on the Strasburg Rail Road (see pages 44–45). *Brian Solomon*

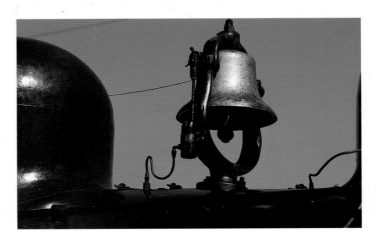

Fresh from a recent overhaul, M&H No. 91 eases out of the shop at Middletown, Pennsylvania, in September 2008. The original M&H was a 6 1/2-mile line chartered in 1888; the present M&H short line began on the eve of Conrail in 1976. *Brian Solomon*

Though the 2-6-0 Mogul type once seemed enormous, old Canadian National No. 89, working at Strasburg, Pennsylvania, today seems tiny compared with the much larger locomotives displayed across the road at the Railroad Museum of Pennsylvania. *Brian Solomon*

Above: No. 89 crosses cornfields on the return leg of an autumn afternoon excursion. Most of the year, the Strasburg Rail Road provides steam-hauled excursions in Pennsylvania Dutch country, making it one of the region's most loved tourist railways. *Brian Solomon*

Left: No. 89 was built in 1910 by the Canadian Locomotive Company for the Grand Trunk Railway. After the GT was melded into the Canadian National Railway in the 1920s, the locomotive served the CNR. Today, it is one of several steam locomotives on the Strasburg Rail Road. *Brian Solomon*

Right: Strasburg Rail Road 2-10-0 No. 90's 56-inch-diameter drivers pound the rails at Strasburg, Pennsylvania. Freight locomotives typically had smaller wheels than those designed for passenger service. Smaller wheels make starting tonnage freights easier, while taller wheels are more effective for operating at higher speeds. *Brian Solomon*

Above: The Strasburg is one of the few railroads in Pennsylvania where steam locomotives operate a regular schedule on a daily basis. *Brian Solomon*

No. 90 has just arrived at the East Strasburg, Pennsylvania, station. This handsome Decapod type was built by Baldwin in 1924 for the Great Western Railway in Loveland, Colorado. In its day as a freight hauler, it moved train loads of sugar beets. It has operated on the Strasburg since 1967. *Brian Solomon*

Above: Popular with enthusiasts, Strasburg No. 475 is not universally liked by crews because of its cramped cab. It has worked at the Strasburg Rail Road since its restoration in 1993. *Brian Solomon*

Right: Norfolk & Western No. 475 once hauled both freight and passenger trains in rural Virginia. Its 21×30-inch cylinders power 56-inch driving wheels. *Brian Solomon*

The 4-8-0 Twelve-Wheeler was not a common type, and the Norfolk & Western had one of the largest rosters in the United States. Old N&W M-class No. 475 was built by Baldwin in 1906 and served in both freight and passenger service for the better part of a half century. On this brisk November afternoon, Strasburg No. 475 approaches the Blackhorse Road crossing at Carpenters on its return run from Lehman Place. *Brian Solomon*

Right: Built by the Grand Trunk's Point St. Charles Shops in April 1921, this classic 0-6-0 switcher was on the Canadian National roster until 1959. (The Grand Trunk became a component of the Canadian National system in 1923.) Since 1971, it has been at North Conway, New Hampshire, where it works on the Conway Scenic Railway. *Brian Solomon*

Above: No. 7470 goes for a spin on the North Conway, New Hampshire, turntable. This locomotive has regularly worked excursions on the Conway Scenic Railway's former Boston & Maine and Maine Central lines in New Hampshire's White Mountains. *Brian Solomon*

Built by the thousands, the 0-6-0 switcher was one of the most common steam locomotives in North America. Typically used for switching freight and passenger cars, the ordinary yard goat didn't attract much attention in the days of steam, but today the Conway Scenic's 0-6-0 No. 7470 is regularly assigned passenger excursions. *Brian Solomon*

Above: Locomotive No. 40 was built by Alco in 1920 for the Portland, Astoria & Pacific. It was briefly owned by the Southern Pacific before going to North Carolina's Aberdine & Rockfish, where it worked for many years. It arrived on Connecticut's Valley Railroad in 1977 and has been entertaining visitors there for three decades. *Brian Solomon*

Right: The 2-8-2 Mikado was based on the successful 2-8-0 Consolidation and 2-6-2 Prairie types. The combination of eight drivers with a comparatively large firebox made it ideal for moving freights, and it became the most popular type of road steam locomotive built in twentieth-century America. *Brian Solomon*

A view down the length of the locomotive from the tender. No. 40's relatively small-diameter drive wheels were typical of branch-line freight locomotives, where traction is more important than speed. *Brian Solomon*

Above: No. 40's conductor guides the engineer using hand signals at Essex, Connecticut. The throttle is open, and with the hiss of steam escaping from cylinders, the engine is just beginning to move. *Brian Solomon*

Right: Brilliant fall foliage makes the Valley Railroad a pleasant seasonal excursion. On its morning run, No. 40 works from Essex toward Deep River. Built as an oil-burner, No. 40 was converted to coal-fired operation in the 1930s. *Brian Solomon*

Morning at Essex, Connecticut, evokes the atmosphere of a small New England station more than 60 years ago. Here, the crew prepares for its run as locomotive No. 40 simmers near the platform. *Brian Solomon*

No. 26 receives nominal maintenance at Steamtown's former Lackawanna Scranton roundhouse. This classic 0-6-0 switcher was built by locomotive manufacturer Baldwin for its own use as a shop switcher. It is one of several locomotives that Steamtown has restored to working order. *Brian Solomon*

Left: The crosshead guides the piston thrust while connecting the piston with the main rod, used to turn the driving wheels. A number of different types of crossheads have been applied over the years. This style, known as the "alligator," was introduced circa 1880. The secondary crosshead connection is part of the valve gear. *Brian Solomon*

Above: No. 26 was constructed in March 1929 for use at Baldwin Locomotive Works' then-recently expanded Eddystone, Pennsylvania, plant. In 1948, Baldwin sold the locomotive to the Jackson Iron and Steel Company in Jackson, Ohio, where it remained through the 1970s. It was acquired by Steamtown in 1986, arriving on the property in Scranton in 1990. The 0-6-0 is one of the most common steam locomotive types preserved in the United States. *George W. Kowanski*

With the Delaware & Hudson's Bernie O'Brien at the throttle, Canadian Pacific No. 2317 charges upgrade with a Steamtown excursion at Hallstead, Pennsylvania. This CPR Class G-3-c Pacific type was built by Montreal Locomotive Works in June 1923 and served for 36 years. It was among the locomotives acquired by the late F. Nelson Blount that have become the core of the Steamtown collection. *George W. Kowanski*

Left: As a regular engine for Steamtown excursions, No. 2317 is familiar to the site's many visitors. Here, the fireman gives a friendly wave on a rainy October day in downtown Scranton. *Brian Solomon*

Above: In July 1995, an evening lineup at Steamtown's former Lackawanna roundhouse finds no fewer than five locomotives under steam. From left to right: Baldwin 0-6-0 No. 26, Canadian National Mikado No. 3254, Canadian Pacific Railway No. 2317, and two visiting locomotives, Blue Mountain & Reading (former Gulf Mobile & Northern) Pacific No. 425 and Lowville & Beaver River Railroad Shay No 8. *George W. Kowanski*

Above: Among the most exciting displays at Scranton's Steamtown National Historic Site are live steam locomotives. In recent years, a regular performer has been Canadian National Mikado No. 3254, which often hauls the demonstration excursion train. *Brian Solomon*

Right: The fireman leans out of the cab of No. 3254 to get a better view along the boiler. Built by the Canadian Locomotive Company at its Kingston (Ontario) Works in 1917, this locomotive originally served the Canadian National's predecessor, the Canadian Government Railways. *Brian Solomon*

Steamtown acquired No. 3254 in 1987 through a trade with the Gettysburg Railroad for Canadian Pacific 4-6-2 No. 1278, which was one of several operable steam locomotives when Steamtown was located at Bellows Falls, Vermont. The collection was moved to Scranton in 1984.
Brian Solomon

Right: East Broad Top No. 12 is the oldest and smallest of the road's Mikado fleet. It is known on the railroad as *Millie.* Brian Solomon

Above: Between 1911 and 1920, the coal-hauling East Broad Top made the unusual step of buying a new fleet of narrow gauge locomotives consisting of six Baldwin Mikados of various sizes. Here, Mikado No. 12 doubleheads with No. 15 on an autumn excursion from Orbisonia to Colgate Grove. *Brian Solomon*

The narrow gauge East Broad Top built south from a connection with the Pennsylvania Railroad at Mt. Union. In August 1873, the EBT reached Orbisonia, 11 miles from Mt. Union. To tap the Broad Top coal fields, the railroad built farther south, reaching Robertsdale in October 1874. By the mid-1950s, its coal traffic had tapped out, and in 1956 the line was abandoned. The railroad was bought by a scrapper that preserved it rather than ripping it up. *Brian Solomon*

Above: East Broad Top Nos. 14 and 15 were built to the same specifications and are 17 tons heavier and slightly more powerful than *Millie* (see pages 62–63), yet smaller than the railroad's heaviest Mikados, Nos. 16, 17 (see pages 66–67), and 18. *Brian Solomon*

Right: Compared with American main lines, which are 4 feet 8 1/2 inches between the rails, the East Broad Top's rails are just 3 feet apart. No. 15 leads an evening excursion downgrade toward Orbisonia. The region's rural charm, combined with the East Broad Top's well-preserved antique railway equipment, has made the railroad a popular attraction since the 1960s. *Brian Solomon*

Leading the first train over the line in nearly a week, No. 15 polishes rusty rails as it works the grade south of Orbisonia on a chilly autumn morning. The sights and sounds of the East Broad Top transport visitors back 80 years to when steam locomotives ruled Pennsylvania's rails.
Brian Solomon

Above: No. 17 is one of the last Mikados built for the East Broad Top and one of the largest on the line. It was capable of hauling 22 steel hoppers with roughly 700 tons of coal up the ruling northbound grade from the mines to Mt. Union. While Nos. 16 and 18 have been cold since the railroad ended common carrier operations in the 1950s, No. 17 made occasional appearances through the 1990s. *Brian Solomon*

Right: The East Broad Top's once-profitable common carrier operations ended in 1956, but a few miles of line were reopened for excursion service in 1960. The railroad occasionally operates freight excursions for the benefit of visitors. Here, No. 17 is fired up for the annual Fall Spectacular. *Brian Solomon*

East Broad Top No. 17 is one of the only surviving locomotives in the United States equipped with the unusual Southern valve-gear arrangement. *Brian Solomon*

On August 4, 1987, Norfolk & Western A-class No. 1218 plies home rails at Bluefield, West Virginia. The N&W A-class were 2-6-6-4 simple articulated types (high-pressure steam to all cylinders) designed for relatively fast running and equipped with roller bearings on all axles. With two sets of cylinders and running gear beneath one boiler, an articulated locomotive effectively comprises two engines worked from a common throttle. *George W. Kowanski*

Left: The N&W concluded heavy steam operations in 1960, several years later than on most American railroads. In the 1980s, No. 1218 was restored to working order, and on August 1, 1987, as part of the National Railroad Historical Society convention, it hauled a train of empty coal hoppers for the delight of photographers.
George W. Kowanski

Above: No. 1218 leads an excursion down 19th Street in Erie, Pennsylvania. The N&W was one of only a few railroads to build its own steam locomotives in the twentieth century. No. 1218 was built in 1943 by the railroad's Roanoke Shops. *Brian Solomon*

Above: The Pennsylvania Railroad's K4s Pacific type was built as a passenger locomotive and became one of the most recognized steam locomotives of its day. For three decades, No. 1361 was displayed at Horseshoe Curve. In 1985, it was removed from its perch and briefly restored to working order. On August 27, 1988, the locomotive emerges from the Howard Tunnel on the old Pennsy Northern Central route. *George W. Kowanski*

Opposite top: To celebrate York's 150th anniversary of railroading, No. 1361 operated seven roundtrips from York, Pennsylvania, to Hanover Junction and Menges Mills between August 26 and 28, 1988. *George W. Kowanski*

Opposite bottom: In 1914, the Pennsylvania Railroad introduced its first Class K4s Pacific. This design was a fusion of the PRR's experimental K29s Pacific and its excellent E6s Atlantic. The K4s proved to be the best passenger locomotive the railroad ever built. The type was mass-produced beginning in 1917, sharing its boiler and other key components with the PRR's L1s Mikado. *George W. Kowanski*

The Pennsylvania Railroad's E2s Atlantics were fast machines. In March 1904, No. 7002 made a special speed run with the PRR claiming it reached 127.1 miles per hour—a record not universally accepted. The PRR scrapped the original 7002 in 1934 and later dressed up another member of the same class, No. 8063, to represent the famous runner. The Railroad Museum of Pennsylvania's second 7002 was operated for a few years in excursion service on the Strasburg Rail Road. *George W. Kowanski*

Left: Although fast, the Atlantic type fell out of favor early because it lacked power to move the longer and heavier trains that emerged with the advent of all-steel passenger cars after 1910. Only a handful of Atlantics have been preserved. Although the second No. 7002 made outings on the Strasburg Rail Road and worked main-line excursions during the 1980s, it is now a static display inside the Railroad Museum of Pennsylvania. *Brian Solomon*

Above: Built by the Pennsylvania Railroad's Juniata Shops at Altoona in 1905, this classic Atlantic type has been dressed with all the period adornment associated with early twentieth-century passenger steam. Note the gold-painted trim on the wheels and tender. In later years, the PRR's locomotives exhibited a more spartan appearance. *George W. Kowanski*

Chapter 2

Trains Across the Plains

Trains Across the Plains

Railroads enabled the rapid settlement and development of the Midwest, where relatively level terrain allowed numerous lines to crisscross the region with relative ease. Locomotive whistles echoing across the cornfields became routine sounds in daily life. Some towns in Ohio, Indiana, and Illinois were served by numerous railway lines that typically crossed each other at grade. Important gateway cities emerged where lines met to interchange freight and where passengers changed trains. The greatest of these gateways was Chicago, which became known as America's railroad capital because of the large numbers of railroads that met there.

Eastern lines, including the Pennsylvania Railroad, New York Central, and Baltimore & Ohio, extended lines to reach Chicago, Cincinnati, and St. Louis. The Nickel Plate Road reached from Buffalo via Cleveland to Chicago and St. Louis. Other railroads began at Chicago and were built westward. Of these, the Santa Fe and the Milwaukee Road ultimately reached the West Coast. Other lines, such as the Chicago & North Western, the Rock Island, and the Burlington, were content to serve the central region.

In the mid-nineteenth century, the 4-4-0 American type developed as the most popular locomotive in North America. As railroads grew busier, the need to haul longer and heavier freight trains and faster and heavier passenger trains spurred locomotive development. New types were developed, both for freight and passenger service, including the 2-6-0 Mogul, which had a greater number of drive wheels than the American type and therefore was better suited for freight. Later, the Mogul became an ideal type for light branch work, serving both freight and passenger trains. The 2-8-0 Consolidation emerged as a standard freight locomotive, built in large numbers during the late nineteenth century and early twentieth century. It was succeeded by the 2-8-2 Mikado, which became the most popular freight locomotive after about 1910.

Passenger locomotives were built more for speed than for hauling heavy tonnage. The 4-6-0 Ten-Wheeler was based on the 4-4-0 American, as was the 4-4-2 Atlantic, with its substantially larger firebox. The 4-6-2 Pacific melded the best of the 4-6-0 and the Atlantic types, and was the most popular passenger steam locomotive of the twentieth century. Some Midwestern railroads were partial to the 2-6-2 Prairie, a type well suited to light lines and level running.

Evermore massive locomotives were built after 1910. Articulated types using two sets of drive wheels on frame that bends laterally, thereby allowing numerous drivers under one boiler to negotiate tight curvature, were desirable on mountain lines and in territory where extremely heavy freights were operated. Although used by some Midwestern lines, articulated types were less common in the Midwest than in the mountains of the East and West.

In the 1920s, the quest for power and speed led to the development of superpower steam. Ohio's Lima Locomotive Works was the pioneer of superpower. While the 2-8-4 Berkshire type was first built for use on the Boston & Albany, several Midwestern railroads, including the Illinois Central and the Nickel Plate Road, were famous for their Berkshires. The 4-6-4 Hudson was developed as a superpower passenger locomotive. The type was used on many lines in the Midwest, including the New York Central, which operated the locomotives to Chicago and St. Louis on its famous passenger trains. The Santa Fe, Burlington, Milwaukee Road, and Canadian Pacific were also known for their Hudsons. A more popular superpower type and one widely embraced all over the United States and by Canadian National—the largest owner of the type—was the 4-8-4. Although often called the Northern type, many railroads objected to this name. The 4-8-4 was well suited to fast freight and fast passenger operations. Relative to the Hudson, which is rare in preservation, a large number of 4-8-4s survived into the diesel age, and several have been used on main-line steam trips in modern times.

There is a great legacy of preserved steam in the central states. A host of museums and preserved lines have displayed and operated steam there, and main-line steam excursions have been relatively common and very popular. In the last 20 years, Milwaukee Road's No. 261, Cotton Belt No. 819, and Union Pacific No. 844—all 4-8-4 types—have been regular visitors on lines in the central part of the country.

Previous pages:
The Nickel Plate Road (NKP) was among the last American railroads to order new steam locomotives and also one of the last to operate large steam in Midwest road-freight service. Several Nickel Plate locomotives have been preserved and operated in main-line excursion service. On May 7, 1980, NKP Berkshire No. 765 worked a freight train on the Toledo, Peoria & Western. *George W. Kowanski*

Above: Milwaukee Road Class S-3 No. 261 is a powerful Northern type built during World War II when the War Production Board limited diesel production and encouraged railroads to acquire new steam power. Minneapolis-based North Star Rail Corporation, in cooperation with The Friends of the 261, regularly operates No. 261 in main-line excursion service. *Brian Solomon*

Right: Milwaukee Road No. 261 works west along the Mississippi River near Savanna, Illinois. The railroad bought its first 4-8-4 in 1930—a Baldwin designed for passenger service. The Milwaukee Road's final order for 4-8-4s was for 10 Alco-built war babies, including No. 261, acquired in 1944 for both freight and passenger service.
Brian Solomon

One of the best seats in railroading is the fireman's position aboard a large steam locomotive.
Brian Solomon

Above: All of the Lackawanna's famous 4-8-4 Poconos were scrapped, so when Steamtown National Historic Site in Scranton, Pennsylvania, wanted to re-create a Pocono for a promotional film, it borrowed Milwaukee Road No. 261 and dressed it up as Lackawanna No. 1661. En route to Pennsylvania on October 11, 1994, the disguised locomotive rolls through Waukesha, Wisconsin, on the Wisconsin Central. *Brian Solomon*

Right: No. 261 makes a run for Milwaukee in the evening twilight. For many years, No. 261 sat as a static display at the National Railroad Museum in Green Bay, Wisconsin, before it was leased and restored by the North Star Rail Corporation in the early 1990s.
Brian Solomon

Heading toward Chicago Union Station on old home rails, Milwaukee Road No. 261 accelerates away from A2 Tower in June 2004. *Brian Solomon*

The first rays of daylight catch Northern Pacific No. 328 under steam at Dresser, Wisconsin, in August 1996. The large horizontal tank above the cylinders and running gear is the air reservoir used for the Westinghouse automatic airbrake. *Brian Solomon*

Above: The Ten-Wheeler type was first built in the 1840s but gained in popularity after the 1860s. Long after the perfection of larger types, this wheel arrangement continued to be built as a dual-service locomotive. Northern Pacific No. 328, built in 1905, is a classic example of a versatile early twentieth-century locomotive. *Brian Solomon*

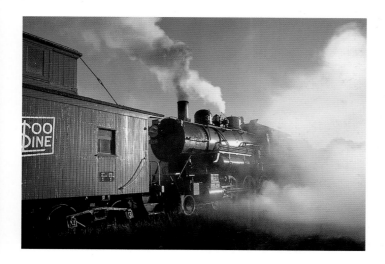

Left: The first rays of sun illuminate Northern Pacific No. 328's exhaust steam as it tows a wooden-sided Soo Line caboose around the wye at Dresser, Wisconsin, on August 17, 1996. *Brian Solomon*

Above: Northern Pacific Class S-10 No. 328 has 57-inch driving wheels that are more or less typical for a locomotive its size. Curiously, this machine was built for the South Manchurian Railway but sold by Alco's Rogers Works to the Northern Pacific in 1907. *Brian Solomon*

Right: A classic Alco-order sand dome sits atop the boiler on Northern Pacific No. 328. This locomotive was restored to operating condition in 1981 and worked for two decades as an excursion engine for the Minnesota Transportation Museum. *Brian Solomon*

As strange as it might seem today, traditional steam-era operating practice only saw headlights switched on when it was dark. *Brian Solomon*

Soo Line No. 1003 was built by Alco in 1913 and enjoyed a remarkably long career. It was retired in 1954 as the railroad was completing its dieselization but was kept in standby service until 1959. On December 17, 2007, the engineer of No. 1003 guides the locomotive on former Milwaukee Road trackage north of Random Lake, Wisconsin. *Chris Guss*

Above: In the 1960s and 1970s, Soo Line No. 1003 was displayed in a park at Superior, Wisconsin. Briefly steamed in the early 1980s, the Class L-1 2-8-2 Mikado was returned to active service in 1996 following an extensive restoration. In a scene that was commonplace across North America more than 60 years ago, No. 1003 passes through the heart of Fredonia, Wisconsin. *Chris Guss*

Left: No. 1003 is one of several serviceable standard gauge Mikados in the United States. Dozens of enthusiasts were on hand to follow No. 1003 on its leisurely jaunt from Plymouth, Wisconsin, on December 15, 2007. The slowly falling snow en route gave the chase a surreal quality, muting most of the landscape surrounding the train and letting the mind wander back to a day when steam ruled the land. *Chris Guss*

89

This Chinese Mikado was the last steam locomotive in the world to roll off a regular assembly line. In 1988, it was sold new to Iowa's Boone & Scenic Valley. Like all steam locomotives, it never fails to capture the enthusiasm of observers. *Brian Solomon*

Above: Boone & Scenic Valley No. JS8419 undergoes its routine morning blow-down procedure on the high trestle west of Boone, Iowa. Blow down is necessary to remove mineral accumulation in the boiler. In the summer, the Boone & Scenic Valley runs weekend trips with the locomotive on its former interurban trackage along the Des Moines River in central Iowa. *Brian Solomon*

Left: A fireman's job is to maintain the fire aboard the locomotive. Although the Boone & Scenic Valley's Chinese Mikado has a mechanical stoker, it is rarely used because the trains are relatively light and there are no challenging grades on the line. *Brian Solomon*

Above: Mikado No. 14 was built by Baldwin in 1913 for the Duluth & Northern Minnesota. In its early years, it worked at Knife River, Minnesota, and was later sold to the Lake Superior & Ishpeming. Since 1981, it has belonged to the Lake Superior Transportation Museum. In July 1996, the locomotive works on the North Shore Scenic Railroad with an excursion toward Two Harbors. *Brian Solomon*

Right: Rods transmit the power of the pistons to the drive wheels, thus converting lateral motion to rotary motion. *Brian Solomon*

No. 14 is bathed in its own steam on an abnormally cool July evening at Duluth after its run to Two Harbors. The locomotive operated in excursion service for several years and last worked in 1998. Today, it is a static display. *Brian Solomon*

This 1901-built Baldwin 2-6-2 once worked for the McCloud River Railroad in California. It is seen here in 1996 on Wisconsin's Kettle Moraine Railway, a popular excursion line operated on a light, isolated, former Milwaukee Road branch line. Sadly, suburban sprawl caught up with the railway and hostility from unsympathetic neighbors was among the reasons for its closing in autumn 2001. The locomotive was donated to the National Railroad Museum at Green Bay, Wisconsin. *Brian Solomon*

Above: The 2-6-2 Prairie type was introduced as a main-line freight locomotive and was briefly tried as a fast passenger engine. Later, it found a niche as a lightweight, branch-line locomotive. The wheel arrangement got its name because of its early popularity with Midwestern granger lines. *Brian Solomon*

Left: Detail of the crosshead and lead driving wheel on the Kettle Moraine Railway No. 9. *Brian Solomon*

The Class R-1 Ten-Wheeler best represents Chicago & North Western (C&NW) steam. In its day, the R-1 was the most common and most versatile type on the railroad. No. 1385 was built by Alco in 1907 and during its long tenure handled a great variety of freight and passenger trains. On a frosty February afternoon, No. 1385 waits at North Freedom, Wisconsin, for the arrival of Saginaw Timber No. 2. *Brian Solomon*

Three C&NW R-1s escaped scrapping. One is preserved at the Forney Transportation Museum in Colorado, and another is privately owned and stored in Upper Michigan. The best known of the three, however, is No. 1385, which resides at the Mid-Continent Railway Museum at North Freedom, Wisconsin. It was operated for a number of years to the thrill of visitors but has been stored since 1998.
Brian Solomon

The old Delaware, Lackawanna & Western never owned a Ten-Wheeler numbered 1061, although it owned a number of Alco-built 4-6-0s in that number series. In 1994, C&NW No. 1385 posed as DL&W 4-6-0 No. 1053 for a Steamtown promotional film.
Brian Solomon

On frigid February 18, 1996, Saginaw Timber Company No. 2 takes on water at North Freedom, Wisconsin. Steam locomotives required lots of water. To keep boilers full, line-side tanks were located at strategic points. *Brian Solomon*

No. 2 is seen through the North Freedom station window. The 2-8-2 Mikado type was developed as a popular freight locomotive in the first decades of the twentieth century. This Baldwin from 1912 was first used by the Saginaw Timber Company and later served a variety of small railroads, including the Polson Lumber Company. In the 1980s, the Mid-Continent Railway Museum restored it to its as-built appearance. *Brian Solomon*

No. 2 makes for a silhouette of steel in a cloud of its own exhaust steam. In the 1990s, the Mid-Continent Railway Museum was blessed with two fine operating steam locomotives. Since 2000, No. 2 has been cold, and now excursions are operated with diesels. Because steam has undeniable appeal for visitors, the museum began raising funds for the restoration of its steam locomotives. *Brian Solomon*

On an overcast afternoon in spring 1968, Nickel Plate Road (NKP) No. 759 leads an excursion near Albany, New York. The 2-8-4 configuration was developed in the mid-1920s by Will Woodard of Lima Locomotive Works for the New York Central's Boston & Albany line, which coined the Berkshire name in honor of the mountains in western Massachusetts. *Richard Jay Solomon*

Above: In the late 1960s and early 1970s, NKP No. 759 was restored to service and operated many public excursions. It even hauled a few freight trains on the Erie Lackawanna and the Western Maryland. On September 12, 1970, it roared west at Newport, Pennsylvania, on the Penn Central's four-track former Pennsylvania Railroad Main Line. Today, No. 759 is a static display at Steamtown in Scranton, Pennsylvania. *George W. Kowanski*

Left: The Nickel Plate Road connected Buffalo and Cleveland with Chicago and St. Louis. The railroad was among the last in the East to work big steam in freight service. However, the railroad barely survived the steam era and in 1964 lost its identity when it was bought by the Norfolk & Western. Today, former Nickel Plate lines are operated by Norfolk Southern, one of the largest railway companies in the East. *Richard Jay Solomon*

The intense traffic demands of World War II placed the Nickel Plate—like all American railroads—in a power crunch. In 1942 and 1943, Lima built 25 Berkshires based on the design of the NKP's S-class 2-8-4s that were built in 1934. Another 30 followed in 1944—in fact, all wartime 2-8-4s were the NKP's Class S-2. After the war, while most lines were buying diesels, the Nickel Plate bucked the trend and bought 10 more Class S-3 Berkshires, built by Lima in 1949. No. 765 is operated by the Fort Wayne (Indiana) Historical Society. *Brian Solomon*

No. 765 works Conrail's multiple-track Niagara Branch near Black Rock, New York. The Berkshire type was the first superpower locomotive, a distinct improvement over earlier designs. The type was built to efficiently haul more freight faster than any previous type. The success of the Berkshire, with its enlarged firebox and boiler, led to a host of new superpower designs. *Brian Solomon*

The first Berkshires that served the Boston & Albany were mountain climbers equipped with driving wheels measuring 63 inches in diameter. By contrast, the Nickel Plate's Berkshires were built for speed and featured 69-inch driving wheels. *Brian Solomon*

103

Nickel Plate Road No. 765 marches through Black Rock in Buffalo, New York, on July 2, 1989.
Brian Solomon

Above: In May 1980, No. 765 makes a show on the Toledo, Peoria & Western at East Peoria, Illinois. Fort Wayne Historical Society's No. 765 operated main-line excursions for many years and completed a thorough restoration in 2005. *George W. Kowanski*

Left: On May 7, 1980, No. 765 shows that it still can do what it was built for as it hauls Toledo, Peoria & Western tonnage across the Illinois Central diamonds at Gilman, Illinois.
George W. Kowanski

In the 1940s and 1950s, the Duluth, Missabe & Iron Range operated enormous Yellowstone articulated types in heavy iron-ore service. DM&IR No. 225 is displayed in a park near DM&IR Proctor Yard in Proctor, Minnesota. *Brian Solomon*

Above: In 1928, the Northern Pacific was the first to adopt the 2-8-8-4 simple articulated locomotive, which it called the Yellowstone type. These were the largest locomotives in the world at the time. The Duluth, Missabe & Iron Range operated a fleet of 18 Baldwin-built Yellowstones. *Brian Solomon*

Left: A street sign in the mining town of Mountain Iron on Minnesota's Iron Range. The DM&IR bought its Yellowstone fleet between 1941 and 1943. They operated as late as 1960, and three have been preserved. *Brian Solomon*

Above: Among the Southern Pacific's affiliated railways was the St. Louis Southwestern, known by its nickname, the Cotton Belt. In October 1988, enthusiasts gather around in admiration of Cotton Belt 4-8-4 No. 819 at Tyler, Texas, with an excursion from Pine Bluff, Arkansas. The Cotton Belt's Class L-1 4-8-4s were built by the railroad's Pine Bluff Shops. *Lewis Raby, courtesy of Tom Kline*

Opposite top: No. 819 storms westward past vintage searchlight signals at Gilmer, Texas, leading an excursion train heading to Tyler, Texas, for the annual Tyler Rose Festival, on October 15, 1993. This magnificent 4-8-4 is maintained in operable condition at Pine Bluff, Arkansas, but has not made main-line trips in recent years. *Tom Kline*

Opposite bottom: Cotton Belt No. 819 charges through the rain on home rails at Buena Vista, Arkansas, on October 16, 1992. This World War II–era locomotive was near 50 years old at the time of the photograph and yet was still capable of maintaining passenger-train speeds. *Tom Kline*

Above: Frisco No. 1522 is a 4-8-2 Mountain type, a wheel arrangement first built in 1911 for passenger service on the Chesapeake & Ohio. The type was later widely adopted across North America for both freight and passenger applications. On September 28, 2002, No. 1522 is seen east of Eureka, Missouri. *Chris Guss*

Right: Working as the star attraction on the Burlington Northern Santa Fe's *Employee Appreciation Special* in May 2001, old Frisco No. 1522 carries a BNSF flag above the markers. The St. Louis & San Francisco was absorbed by the Burlington Northern in 1980, decades after it dumped the fires on its last steam locomotives. *Tom Kline*

Working east at the end of the day, Frisco No. 1522 is east of Newberg, Missouri. *Chris Guss*

The Southern Pacific, including its lines in Mexico, operated a total of 164 2-8-2 Mikados, a relatively small number considering the size of the railroad. By comparison, it had far larger fleets of 2-6-0, 4-6-0, and 2-8-0 types. Of its Mikados, five were set aside for preservation, including No. 786, which sat on display at Austin, Texas, for years until its restoration in 1991. *Tom Kline*

No. 786 was built by Alco at the former Brooks Locomotive Works in Dunkirk, New York, in 1916 and is representative of the Southern Pacific Mikados, featuring 63-inch driving wheels and 200-psi boiler pressure. Mikados were workhorse locomotives. Although often assigned to freight, some worked passenger trains, especially this engine, which spent its years on the railroad's Texas and Louisiana lines. *Tom Kline*

On a clear but frigid winter morning, engineer Joe Dale Morris, who at the time was the general manager of the Austin Steam Train Association, looks back from the cab of Southern Pacific No. 786 to inspect his train at Bertram, Texas, on November 22, 1992. The train, known as the *Hill Country Flyer*, operates between Cedar Park (near Austin) and Burnett, Texas, on a former SP line that was purchased by the city of Austin. *Tom Kline*

Chapter 3
Taming the West

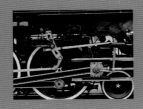

Taming the West

Railroads in the West followed a distinct developmental pattern different from that of the rest of the country. While railroads in the East tended to connect existing communities and serve industry, the early lines in the West were built across hundreds of miles of unsettled and undeveloped land, and required large federal subsidies to encourage and finance construction. Light population densities and vast distances resulted in fewer lines than elsewhere in the country. Except for a few established locations, such as Denver, Salt Lake City, and San Francisco, many western communities owe their founding to the coming of the railroad.

Western railroads were built to handle transcontinental traffic, serve regional agriculture (including the cattle and timber trades), and tap mineral resources. A handful of large railroads dominated the scene, but there were dozens of smaller lines.

Geographical characteristics of western lines affected locomotive development in a variety of ways. Western railroads tended to be heavily graded, often with steep, prolonged climbs. As a result, railroads sought evermore powerful machines. In the nineteenth century, the Central Pacific/Southern Pacific pushed the limits of design by building and buying a significant number of 4-8-0 Twelve-Wheelers and manufacturing the only known 4-10-0 in a failed effort to increase power. Between 1902 and 1904, the Santa Fe expanded the 2-10-0 Decapod by adding trailing trucks, resulting in the 2-10-2 Santa Fe type. (The Southern Pacific bought large numbers of 2-10-2s in the 1910s and 1920s but refused to acknowledge the name of their competitor, referring to the type as "Decks.")

Various specialized articulated types were common on western lines, and the Great Northern was the first to buy articulated Mallet (named for Swiss mechanical engineer Anatole Mallet, and pronounced "mallay") compounds for road service, ordering 2-6-6-2s from Baldwin in 1906. (The first North American railroad to use the Mallet was the Baltimore & Ohio, which two years earlier had adapted it as a helper locomotive.) For better service on Donner Pass, where smoke was a problem in snow sheds and long tunnels, the Southern Pacific reversed the articulated type, moving the cab forward.

Other railroads built some of the largest steam locomotives in the world to handle greater amounts of tonnage. The largest in the West was the Union Pacific's 4-8-8-4 Big Boy of 1941, a type expanded from the already enormous 4-6-6-4 Challenger.

Not all of the West's giant steam locomotives were articulated types, however. In the 1920s, the Union Pacific had originated the 4-10-2 Overland type and expanded this locomotive to the 4-12-2 Union Pacific type, featuring the longest rigid wheelbase of any locomotive ever constructed. The Northern Pacific was first to adopt the 4-8-4, which it called the Northern type, while another articulated type, the 2-10-4, was known as the Texas type.

Among the other distinctive characteristics of many western railroads was the choice of fuel. From the late nineteenth century onward, most railroads in the East burned coal. The dearth of accessible coal on the other side of the continent, however, led to the development of oil-burning steam locomotives in the far West. The Santa Fe pioneered the oil-burner, and by the first decades of the twentieth century, most railroads on the West Coast were using oil-burning steam locomotives.

The crucial role of the railroad in developing the West has played an important part in locomotive preservation. Western communities have been well aware of the importance of the steam locomotive, and in the 1950s, western railroads were exceptionally generous in donating examples of their locomotives to towns and cities along their lines. While a great many smaller locomotives—0-6-0s, 2-8-0s, and the like—found their way into town parks, a number of larger machines were preserved. The Southern Pacific's famous No. 4449 was displayed for a number of years in a city park in Portland, Oregon, before being restored to service in the mid-1970s for the American Freedom Train. The Union Pacific not only preserved many of its locomotives, but also retained some for its own use. No. 844, for example, was never dropped from the roster and has continued to run since it was built in 1944.

The popularity of the Rio Grande narrow gauge resulted in one of America's first tourist railways, the Durango & Silverton, and contributed to the preservation in 1970 of the Antonito, Colorado–to–Chama, New Mexico, segment of the Rio Grande as the Cumbres & Toltec Scenic Railroad. Both lines operate with former Rio Grande 2-8-2 Mikados.

Previous pages:
The Rio Grande's narrow gauge Silverton Branch was built to tap mine traffic. The railroad tried to abandon the line in the 1950s, but interest in its steam-hauled passenger trains spurred a revival as a tourist hauler. The growth in passenger ridership proved profitable, and the Rio Grande began to promote steam trains as a tourist attraction. Brightly painted passenger cars and an Old West theme were used to attract visitors. Former Rio Grande Class K-36 No. 482 leads an excursion northward through Beaver Creek Canyon, Colorado, in September 1995. *Tom Kline*

Southern Pacific No. 4449, a streamlined 4-8-4 Class GS-4 built by Lima, has become one of the most famous locomotives in America. In 1991, it worked an excursion to Railfair Sacramento from Portland, Oregon. Here, the locomotive works hard at Ericson, California, with a long consist of *Daylight*-painted passenger cars in tow. *Brian Solomon*

Left: The stylized *Daylight* insignia was designed by Charles L. Eggleston and introduced in 1937 for SP's new streamlined trains between San Francisco and Los Angeles. The *Daylight* scheme incorporated colors associated with California. *Daylight* orange is a near match to the hue of the California poppy, while the golden connotation harks back to the gold rush. *Tom Kline*

Above: The GS-4 was the zenith of the Southern Pacific's Northern types. In 1941, Lima built 28 of them—Nos. 4430 to 4457. Of these, only No. 4449 survives. Here, No. 4449 leads an excursion across the Sacramento River at Redding, California. *Brian Solomon*

In May 1991, Southern Pacific No. 4449 leads an eastward excursion along the shore of San Pablo Bay near Pinole, California. In the Southern Pacific classification system, 4-8-4 types were classified "GS," for "general service" or "Golden State." *Brian Solomon*

Looking much like it did back in the 1940s, No. 4449 works upgrade on home rails at Worden, Oregon, on its way to Sacramento on April 28, 1991.
Brian Solomon

Although impressive when observed from a distance, the enormous size of a steam locomotive is most evident when you get up close. No. 4449 rests at Redding, California, before making a run to Black Butte and back.
Brian Solomon

Southern Pacific No. 4449 was one of three steam locomotives recruited to haul the American Freedom Train, a patriotic exercise designed to coincide with the American Bicentennial in 1976. The train carried historical artifacts and toured the continental United States for millions to see.
George W. Kowanski

Left: Streamlined No. 4449 awes young observers. When styling the *Daylight*, the Southern Pacific left no detail untouched. Even elements such as the pilot were given the *Daylight* treatment. *Brian Solomon*

Above: Two generations of Southern Pacific passenger steam: On the left is Baldwin-built P-8 Pacific-type No. 2472, one of 15 locomotives delivered in 1921; on the right is No. 4449, built in 1941. When new, both types represented the best of the railroad's passenger power. Today, these classics inspire nostalgia for passenger trains that once connected California cities with those across the southwestern United States. *Brian Solomon*

In spring 1991, the Southern Pacific's Class P-8 No. 2472 and GS-4 No. 4449 lead a Railfair Sacramento excursion along the shore of San Pablo Bay at Pinole, California. *Brian Solomon*

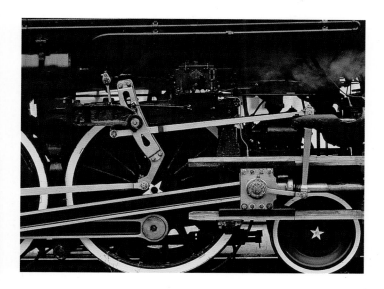

This detail of No. 2472 shows the crosshead, main rod, valve gear, and driving wheels. Part of the attraction of steam locomotives is that the majority of the operating equipment is out in the open for all to see. *Brian Solomon*

No. 2472 is a Class P-8 Pacific type built by Baldwin in 1921. Like many twentieth-century Southern Pacific steam locomotives, it's an oil-burner. *Brian Solomon*

Popular with railway enthusiasts, No. 2472 made an extended visit to the Niles Canyon Railway in 2008. In this view, it pulls an excursion train toward Sunol, California. *Brian Solomon*

Above: In August 1992, restored No. 2472 leads an eastward excursion on the Coast Line near Harlem, California. This handsome locomotive has thrilled thousands in excursion service since 1991 and is one of a few active Pacific types in the United States. *Brian Solomon*

Left: The SP's Pacific types were standard main-line passenger power in the 1920s and 1930s. The P-8s survived to the end of steam, working in secondary services, and were retired in the 1950s. In April 1991, No. 2472 is seen at Oakland's Jack London Square on its maiden run following restoration. *Brian Solomon*

Right: No. 3 was built by Lima in 1912 for the Alaculsy Lumber Company in Tennessee. In 1945, it worked for the Coal Processing Corporation at Dixiana, Virginia, from which it got its name. Since 1962, No. 3 has served as a tourist locomotive at the Roaring Camp & Big Trees at Felton, California, where it brings visitors over a re-created narrow gauge logging railroad. *Brian Solomon*

Above: Built in the 1960s, California's Roaring Camp & Big Trees emulates steeply graded, timber-hauling, narrow gauge lines common in California in the early twentieth century. Grades reach 10 percent—a rise of 10 feet for every 100 traveled—impossibly steep for conventional steam locomotives but easily conquered by geared steam. *Brian Solomon*

Conventional reciprocating rod–driven steam locomotives were ineffective for industrial applications, where poor track, steep grades, and slow operating speeds were the norm. Filling this gap were steam locomotives with geared drives, the most popular of which was the Shay type, named for its designer, lumberman Ephraim Shay, and built by Lima. Roaring Camp & Big Trees No. 3, named *Dixiana*, is typical of a two-truck Shay used in lumber service. *Brian Solomon*

Above: No. 28 is a handsome 2-8-0 Consolidation type built by Baldwin in 1922 for the Sierra Railway. When No. 28 eases out of the yard at Jamestown, California, it's doing so on home rails. Except for infrequent displays in Sacramento, old No. 28 has never worked off line. *Brian Solomon*

Right: Before a day of excursion work, Sierra Railway No. 28 comes up to pressure inside the railway's vintage 1910 roundhouse, one of the last in the western United States. Today, the historic Sierra Railway—a part of Railtown 1897, managed by the California State Railroad Museum—operates seasonal weekend steam and diesel excursions using trackage rights on 3 miles of Sierra Railroad. *Brian Solomon*

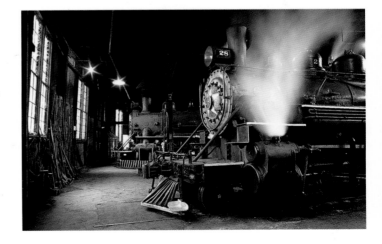

The Sierra Railway has been a choice location for film and television for decades, and old No. 28 has starred in several productions. Yet, this 2-8-0 is not an exceptional machine, but rather typical of moderately sized locomotives of its period. *Brian Solomon*

No. 18 has had an unusual history. It left the Baldwin Locomotive Works in 1912 for the McCloud River Railroad, where it worked until 1956. Its revenue freight work behind it, the Mikado was sold to the nearby Yreka Western short line for a brief excursion service career that ended in the early 1960s. In 1998, the McCloud bought the locomotive back, restoring it to service in 2001, only to sell it a few years later. It's seen here in March 2008, operating a trip on the Sierra Railroad out of Oakdale, California. *John Gruber*

Left: No. 18 breathes steam into the cool morning air as it is prepared at Oakdale, California, for an excursion on the Sierra Railroad. *John Gruber*

Above: McCloud River Railroad Baldwin Mikado No. 18 is coupled with the Sierra Railroad's S12 Baldwin switcher No. 42 at Oakdale, California. *John Gruber*

This Baldwin 2-6-0 Mogul type was built by Baldwin for the Southern Pacific in 1901. At the time of its construction, compounding was a popular system for reducing operating costs, and No. 1744 was among a number of SP locomotives built as a four-cylinder Vauclain compound, in which high-pressure cylinders exhausted into low-pressure cylinders to make double use of the steam. The savings proved illusory, as high maintenance costs canceled out efficiency gains. No. 1744, along with many other compounds, was rebuilt as the conventional simple engine pictured here. *George W. Kowanski*

In the 1980s, No. 1744 was a regular excursion engine on the Heber Creeper, a tourist railway operating on a former Rio Grande standard gauge branch in Utah. In 2008, the tourist line was known as the Heber Valley Railroad, while No. 1744 was working excursions on another former Rio Grande line hundreds of miles away. *George W. Kowanski*

Earl Knoob replaces a burned-out lamp on No. 1744, working in Rio Grande Scenic Railroad excursion service on the San Luis & Rio Grande. This classic Mogul was one of two steam locomotives used to haul trains up the standard gauge La Veta Pass in recent years. *Tom Kline*

Above: No. 346 was built in July 1881 by Baldwin for the Denver & Rio Grande Railway, a predecessor of what would become the Denver & Rio Grande Western Railroad. Originally, it was numbered 406 and named *Cumbres*. It is preserved in working order at the Colorado Railroad Museum at Golden. *Brian Solomon*

Right: While most of the operable Rio Grande narrow gauge steam locomotives are twentieth-century 2-8-2 Mikados, No. 346 is a 2-8-0 and is a generation older than the earliest narrow gauge Mikados. It had nearly a half century of operation by the time the last D&RGW Mikados were delivered. *Brian Solomon*

In 1870, the Denver & Rio Grande's William Jackson Palmer sailed to Great Britain for an extended honeymoon. There, he inspected the 2-foot-gauge slate-hauling Festiniog Railway in North Wales and met leading narrow gauge proponents who advised Palmer to adopt narrow gauge. The Rio Grande's first locomotive was a 2-4-0, but it soon adopted larger types. *Brian Solomon*

Above: The Rio Grande's K-27s—popularly known as "Mudhens"—were the first locomotives built with outside frames, along with outside counterweights and crankpins. No. 463 works as a helper ahead of a K-36 with a train that has just reached the summit of Cumbres Pass, Colorado, on the Cumbres & Toltec Scenic Railroad. *Brian Solomon*

Right: Mudhens were the smallest of the D&RG's Mikados, yet were considered enormous by narrow gauge standards of the day. No. 463 is under steam at Chama, New Mexico. *Brian Solomon*

The Cumbres & Toltec Scenic Railroad's heavy excursion trains require a helper from Chama, New Mexico, up the 4 percent grade to Cumbres Pass. No. 463 is a head-end helper that has paused at Cresco tank for water. Before World War I, the Denver & Rio Grande upgraded the west slope of Cumbres Pass with heavier track to permit operation of K-27s as helpers. *Brian Solomon*

Right: Most of the Denver & Rio Grande Western's twentieth-century narrow gauge steam locomotives were Baldwin products. The exceptions were the 10 Class K-28 Mikados built by Alco in 1923. Known popularly as "Sport Models," these locomotives—including No. 478—were regularly assigned to passenger trains. No. 478 leads a Durango & Silverton excursion at Silverton, Colorado. *Brian Solomon*

Above: During World War II, seven D&RGW K-28s were sent to the White Pass & Yukon in Alaska, where they served for a short time. After the war, they were scrapped. The three surviving K-28s now operate on the Durango & Silverton. A pair of K-28s doublehead on a northward excursion train in Colorado's Animas River Canyon in 1995. *Tom Kline*

No. 478 at Durango, Colorado, August 1991. D&RGW's Silverton Branch traffic had largely tapped out by the 1950s, but tourist ridership was profitable, so the line evolved into one of the first modern tourist railways. The line was later sold off, creating the Durango & Silverton. *Brian Solomon*

In 1925, the Denver & Rio Grande Western ordered an additional 10 outside-frame Class K-36 Mikados from Baldwin. The Rio Grande's K-36 Mikados were the last all-new narrow gauge locomotives built for the railroad. *Tom Kline*

Above: No. 481 leads an excursion on a narrow shelf high above the Animas River. Each of the Rio Grande's four classes of narrow gauge Mikados featured a distinct number sequence. The K-27s were numbered in the 450s and 460s, K-28s in the 470s, K-36s in the 480s, and K-37s in the 490s. *Brian Solomon*

Left: No. 481 leads a returning excursion toward Durango, Colorado, on a clear summer afternoon. *Brian Solomon*

Above: A mechanic attaches a blue flag to Durango & Silverton No. 482. The blue flag is the most restrictive signal on a railroad. It prevents a piece of equipment from being moved, and the signal can only be removed by the employee who places it. *Tom Kline*

Opposite top: Alco-built K-28 No. 478 and Baldwin K-36 No. 482 rest at Silverton, Colorado, after making their run along the Animas River from Durango. At one time, Silverton was an important railway hub where mining lines fed the Denver & Rio Grande Western. Today, it's the end of the line. *Tom Kline*

Opposite bottom: No. 482 catches the sun as it climbs through Pinkerton, Colorado, on September 20, 1995. The Durango & Silverton is among the most popular excursion railways in the West. *Tom Kline*

The Cumbres & Toltec Scenic Railroad operates an excursion line using the former Denver & Rio Grande Western San Juan extension between Antonito, Colorado, and Chama, New Mexico. Here, C&TS K-36 No. 487 works the grade over Cumbres Pass, one of the highest remaining lines in North America. *Brian Solomon*

Cumbres & Toltec's former Rio Grande No. 487 carries a removable plow. Beneath the plow is a more typical pilot such as that seen on sister K-36 No. 481 (see pages 140–141). *Brian Solomon*

After a day's service, the fireman and engineer of No. 487 converse in the cab at Chama, New Mexico. The locomotive was built in 1925. In 1970, it was conveyed, along with 64 miles of former Rio Grande trackage, to the Cumbres & Toltec Scenic Railroad, which is jointly owned by the states of Colorado and New Mexico. *Brian Solomon*

To permit a significantly larger and more powerful narrow gauge locomotive, the Rio Grande's Mikados required a specialized design featuring outside frames, crankpins, and counterweights instead of the arrangement typical of standard gauge locomotives. Introduced with K-27s in 1903, this design was last applied to the K-37s that the railroad rebuilt from standard gauge 2-8-0s between 1928 and 1930. *Brian Solomon*

Above: Rio Grande K-37 No. 497 leads a Cumbres & Toltec photo freight near Big Horn, New Mexico, in September 1999. After years of decline, Rio Grande abandoned its San Juan extension in 1969. By that time, freight operations had become sporadic and the railroad had greatly deteriorated. The exceptionally scenic 64-mile section along the Toltec Gorge and over Cumbres Pass was preserved by the states of Colorado and New Mexico as the Cumbres & Toltec Scenic Railroad. While C&TS typically operates passenger excursions, occasionally it runs period freights for photographers. *Tom Kline*

Left: No. 497 works from Chama to the summit at Cumbres Pass. This grueling climb is one of the best places to find steam locomotives working in North America.
Brian Solomon

The locomotive *Sonoma*, engine No. 12, is a classic wood-burner adorned in the style typical of engines built in the mid-Victorian period. Polished Russian iron boiler plate, ornate brass fittings, and detailed paintwork were among the trademarks of this period. In the 1930s, it was recognized as an antique gem and set aside for preservation. Today, it is beautifully restored and displayed at the California State Railroad Museum in Sacramento. *Brian Solomon*

No. 12 is a nicely proportioned narrow gauge 4-4-0 American type built by Baldwin in 1876 for California's North Pacific Coast, a railway built to connect ferry piers at Sausalito with timber stands along the Russian River Valley. After a few years, it was sold and spent most of its operating life on the Nevada Central Railway. Today, it is beautifully restored and displayed at the California State Railroad Museum in Sacramento. *Brian Solomon*

Baldwin builder's plate on the North Pacific Coast's No. 12. *Brian Solomon*

Above: The Eureka & Palisade's No. 4 *Eureka* is a classic 3-foot-gauge 4-4-0 built by Baldwin in July 1875. For years, this beautiful locomotive was owned by Warner Bros. for use in motion pictures. Today, it is privately owned and usually stored near Las Vegas, Nevada. *Tom Kline*

Right: No. 4 has made an occasional appearance on the Durango & Silverton. A lightweight compared with the massive machines of the twentieth century, No. 4 weighs just 22 1/2 tons—almost 1/17 the weight of a Union Pacific Big Boy. *Tom Kline*

The *Eureka* is a near cousin to the *Sonoma* preserved at the California State Railroad Museum (see pages 148–149). Both 4-4-0s were built as wood-burners and lushly adorned in the ornate style of the period. *Tom Kline*

The Union Pacific's 800 4-8-4s were fast and powerful engines designed to operate with a 1,000-ton passenger train at a sustained 90 miles per hour. Union Pacific No. 844—the last in its class—not only escaped retirement, but has operated nearly every year since it rolled out of Alco's Schenectady, New York, plant in 1944. In August 1996, it worked east to Chicago over the former Chicago & North Western main line. *Brian Solomon*

Left: Today, No. 844 is one of very few American steam locomotives still owned and operated by the railroad that bought it. In September 1989, it took a break from excursion service to haul a grain train to Cheyenne, Wyoming. It is pictured here climbing Archer Hill. *Brian Solomon*

Above: During the years when the Union Pacific had GP30 No. 844, its preserved 4-8-4 carried an extra "4." In April 1981, Union Pacific Nos. 8444 and 3985 lead an excursion over the Southern Pacific's Donner Pass on their way to Railfair Sacramento. The train has just exited Tunnel No. 7 and is about to enter Tunnel No. 6 at Donner Summit. The trackage here was part of the original 1868 Donner crossing, built as part of the first transcontinental railroad. *George W. Kowanski*

Union Pacific No. 3985 leads an excursion to San Jose over Altamont Pass in 1992. The UP's 4-6-6-4 Challengers were among the most successful high-speed articulated types, combining the benefits of a four-wheel leading truck and tall driving wheels with contemporary innovations for better stability at higher speeds. *Brian Solomon*

The Union Pacific's Bob Krieger holds No. 3985's engineer's seat during a switching move. This popular locomotive has operated in excursion service across the UP's vast western network. *Tom Kline*

The Union Pacific's Challengers were designed for speeds of 70 miles per hour. These huge, powerful machines offered operational flexibility as a result of articulation and exceptional power. As of 2008, No. 3985 was the largest operating locomotive in the world. *Brian Solomon*

Union Pacific No. 3985 leads an excursion eastward at Peru, Wyoming, on June 28, 1982. The Challenger type was designed by the Union Pacific's assistant general superintendent Otto Jablemann. The first of the type was built by Alco in 1936. Built in 1943, No. 3985 was part of the final order for the type. *George W. Kowanski*

Left: Fireman Rick Braunschweig has his hand on the injector lever and his eye on the sight glass as water fills No. 3985's enormous boiler at Trinity, Texas, in June 2004. *Tom Kline*

Above: Under sunny skies on June 14, 1993, No. 3985 and DDA40X No. 6936 climb eastward at Quartz with the *Oregon Trail Special*. Eastern Oregon is famous for its heavily graded UP main line. This is the west slope of Encina Hill, just a few miles east of Baker City. In the distance are the snow-crested peaks of the Blue Mountains. *Brian Solomon*

Chapter 4

Steam in Europe

Steam in Europe

The locomotive developed differently in Britain than it did in North America. The more restrictive loading gauge in Britain required more compact locomotive design. Not only did British steam locomotives tend to be smaller, lower, and shorter than their American counterparts, they appeared neater because various appliances and equipment were kept within tighter confines. British steam locomotives were built with inside cylinders and inside valve gear decades after this style was abandoned in North America. Outside valve gear, common in America after 1910, was not widely adopted by British designs for another generation. Further, American locomotives were largely free from extraneous adornment after about 1885, but British locomotives continued to feature decorative trappings until the 1940s.

Most of Britain's railways were grouped into the "Big Four" companies in 1923. The London, Midland & Scottish Railway, the Great Western Railway, the London & North Eastern Railway, and the Southern Railway were regional systems that operated the bulk of the British railway network until the system was nationalized in 1947. British Railways, as the unified system was called, stuck with steam a decade longer than its U.S. counterparts. Britain's last steam locomotive, *Evening Star*, was built in 1960—the same year main-line steam operations ended in the United States. Main-line steam in Britain continued until 1968.

Britain has recognized its steam legacy and today offers some of the world's finest preserved railways with dozens of locomotives kept in working order. The great variety of preserved railways allows visitors to experience many types of locomotives working in diverse settings and applications. The Great Central Railway in Leicestershire has rebuilt a section of former main line, including a significant portion of double track. There, several locomotives may be working the line at one time, creating an aura of big-time operations reminiscent of the 1950s when steam ruled British rails. The Severn Valley Railway (SVR) has re-created the atmosphere of a secondary line, featuring several small stations and operating through its bucolic, namesake valley. In season, this 16-mile-long railway operates a regular passenger service that connects at Kidderminster with main-line passenger services. It is not unusual to find five or more locomotives under steam on the SVR. Of a similar concept, although not as extensive, is the Keighley & Worth Valley, a 5-mile line that connects its namesake points and retains all the flavor of a British branch line.

Wales is famous for its narrow gauge railways, of which the Festiniog is the best known. This former slate-hauling line uses tracks just 1 foot 11 1/2 inches wide and operates a number of classic locomotives, including articulated Fairlie types. Affiliated with the Festiniog is the Welsh Highland Railway that operates Garratt locomotives, a type never used in the United States. Instead of the conventional rigid frame and the boiler riding atop the running gear, a Garratt type features a boiler suspended on the frame between two sets of articulated running gear, thus enabling the use of a large boiler on a narrow gauge locomotive.

Ireland's railways were built by British engineers in the Victorian period and used locomotives either built by British manufacturers or largely influenced by British designs. Unlike railways in Britain, North America, and most of continental Europe, Ireland's railways are largely broad gauge— 5 feet 3 inches between the rails. Ireland began buying large numbers of diesel-electric locomotives in the 1950s, and by 1963 the conversion from steam power was complete. Today, the Railway Preservation Society of Ireland routinely operates main-line excursions with historic steam locomotives over both the Irish Rail and the Northern Ireland Railways.

Steam power may be experienced in a number of countries on the European continent. Among regular operations are Austria's narrow gauge Zillertalbahn, operating between Jenbach and Mayrhofen, and Polish National Railways, known for maintaining the last standard gauge steam roundhouse in Europe in daily operation. Also noteworthy are several narrow gauge steam operations in Germany, where standard gauge steam is occasionally used for main-line excursions. In addition, steam-hauled trains are sometimes used for regular services in what Germans refer to as plandampfs, or "timetabled steam."

Previous pages:
The quiet fields of County Wexford in Ireland are momentarily disturbed by the puff-puff-puff of Great Southern & Western Railway No. 186 as it slowly climbs Taylorstown bank between Wellingtonbridge and Ballycullane on its way to Waterford. *Brian Solomon*

Under a good head of steam, the West Country Pacific type *Boscastle* leads an excursion on Britain's preserved Great Central Railway in Leicestershire. The Southern Railway had 66 West Country Pacifics. *Brian Solomon*

Above: Between 1923 and 1947, Britain's Southern Railway operated most of the lines south of London. Southern chief mechanical officer O. V. S. Bulleid had worked under Sir Nigel Gresley on the London North Eastern Railway and continued to refine Gresley's concepts on the Southern's Pacific types in the 1940s. Bulleid's West Country light Pacifics were introduced in 1945. Locomotive No. 34039 *Boscastle* is a modified West Country type that has had much of its original streamlined shrouding removed. *Brian Solomon*

Left: The West Country Pacifics have a similar appearance to Bulleid's Merchant Navy class. Both were considered compact machines compared with those built for American railroads. They were just 12 feet 11 inches tall and 67 feet 4 3/4 inches long, including the tender. By contrast, a Pennsylvania Railroad K4s Pacific measured 74 feet 8 inches long. *Brian Solomon*

Marching upgrade in heavy rain, the Southern Railway's West Country Pacific No. 21C123, *Blackmoor Vale*, leads an excursion on the Bluebell Railway. This preserved line south of London operates 9 miles of a former Southern Railway secondary main line that was trimmed from the network in the 1960s. *Brian Solomon*

Left: Blackmoor Vale looks very much the way the West Country Pacific class appeared when new back in 1945. It features the full streamlining treatment and is painted in the Southern's Malachite green. Here, it approaches Horsted Keynes on the preserved Bluebell Railway. *Brian Solomon*

Above: Blackmoor Vale was one of many British steam locomotives rescued from a scrapper in South Wales during the 1960s and 1970s. Operational British steam survived on a wider scale much later than in America, but the transition to other modes was more rapid. The last revenue steam disappeared in August 1968. *Brian Solomon*

The London, Midland & Scottish Railway's chief mechanical officer, W. A. Stanier, was well known for his exceptionally good locomotive designs. His Class 5 4-6-0, popularly known as the Black Five, was the most numerous locomotive type built in twentieth-century Britain. Preserved Black Five No. 45110 passes mechanically operated semaphores at Bewdley on Britain's Severn Valley Railway. *Brian Solomon*

Dressed in the British Railways' livery of the 1950s, Black Five No. 45110 works on the Severn Valley Railway. The Black Five was introduced in Britain the same year that the Burlington's diesel-powered *Zephyr* made its debut in America. The *Zephyr* was retired in 1960 after spawning widespread interest in dieselization, while Britain built its last steam locomotive that same year. Some of the Black Fives worked right to the end of steam in 1968. *Brian Solomon*

The 4-6-0 was a popular type on the London, Midland & Scottish Railway prior to the design of the Black Five in 1934. When LMS was formed in 1923, it inherited more than 800 4-6-0s from predecessor companies. The success of Stanier's Black Five not only led to mass production, but made it the platform for British Rail's 5MT design built from 1951 to 1957. *Brian Solomon*

Best known of the Great Western Railway's 4-6-0s was its celebrated King class capable of sustained high-speed running. By contrast, No. 7812, *Erlestoke Manor*, is an example of the GWR's Manor class, a type derived from the Grange class 4-6-0 and specifically for use on lighter lines. No. 7812 approaches Bewdley on a former GWR line preserved by the Severn Valley Railway. *Brian Solomon*

No. 7812 pauses with an excursion train at Arley on the Severn Valley Railway, a preserved line more than 16 miles long that is home to a variety of restored steam locomotives. Arley is one of several active stations on the line that retain the character of an age gone by. *Brian Solomon*

Driving wheels of No. 7812, *Erlestoke Manor*, one of three GWR Manor class 4-6-0s preserved on the Severn Valley Railway. Thirty of this class were built between 1930 and 1950. Relatively light axle weight with good pulling characteristics made them ideal for passenger service on lightly built secondary lines. This locomotive dates to 1939. *Brian Solomon*

Above: From 1923 until nationalization of British Railways in 1947, the London, Midland & Scottish Railway served the territory described by its name. LMS Class 8F 2-8-0s were built beginning in 1935 for freight services. No. 48431 was photographed on the preserved Keighley & Worth Valley Railway. *Brian Solomon*

Opposite top: The 8F was among the best locomotives designed by the LMS's Sir William Stanier. It was mass-produced by no less than 11 different locomotive works in Britain. In addition to those locomotives serving the LMS and later British Railways, the type was exported to Italy and Middle Eastern countries. No. 48431 works upgrade toward the Mytholmes Tunnel near Haworth on the Keighley & Worth Valley Railway. *Brian Solomon*

Opposite bottom: The Worth Valley is best known as home to the famous Brontë sisters. Today, visitors also come to ride heritage trains, such as this one led by No. 48431. *Brian Solomon*

In 1936, the London & North Eastern Railway's highly praised chief mechanical officer, Sir Nigel Gresley (best known for his adaptation and perfection of the 4-6-2 Pacific type to British practice) applied his expert guidance in the development of a modern 2-6-2 type. The V2 prototype, class leader No. 4771, was built by the LNER's Doncaster Works in 1936. The type was deemed successful, and between 1936 and 1944, the LNER built a fleet of 184 V2s, dividing construction between its Doncaster and Darlington Works. *Brian Solomon*

Above: The LNER's pioneer V2, No. 4771, was named *Green Arrow* after the railway's fast freight service marketed under the same name. While such naming occasionally perplexes modern-day observers, at the time the naming logic was implicit, since the class V2 was designed to work fast freight. During World War II, the V2 class proved its value. The *Green Arrow* was preserved and still occasionally works main-line excursions. *Brian Solomon*

Left: The V2 was a three-cylinder simple locomotive. One key to its success was the casting of all three cylinders in a monoblock featuring carefully designed steam passages to ease flow of steam to the pistons. The central cylinder drove a crank axle. To reduce destructive dynamic forces, the V2 used lightweight alloyed-steel drive rods with precision counterbalanced drive wheels and reciprocating equipment. The last of the class was retired at the end of 1966. *Brian Solomon*

One of Britain's Big Four railways formed in 1923, the Southern Railway operated lines south and southwest of London. R. E. L. Maunsell, the Southern's first chief mechanical engineer, designed a number of 2-6-0s for passenger services, including the U class (Nos. 1610 to 1639). No. 1638 is a regular on the Bluebell Railway, one of the United Kingdom's pioneer preserved lines. Here, No. 1638 is seen ready to depart Sheffield Park with the Bluebell's high-end dining train, styled the *Golden Arrow* after the Southern's traditional continental express of the same name. *Brian Solomon*

Above: The Bluebell Railway was the first standard gauge preserved line in Britain and has rebuilt 9 miles of former Southern Railway secondary main line in East Sussex between Sheffield Park and Kingscote. Its premier excursion service is an all-Pullman dining train named after the Southern's *Golden Arrow*, seen here led by No. 1638 climbing the grade north of Horsted Keynes. The *Golden Arrow* re-creates a classic railway atmosphere for day-trippers visiting the line. *Brian Solomon*

Left: No. 1638 was built in 1931 and is one of two U-class 2-6-0s preserved on the Bluebell Railway. Bluebell, like most of Britain's finest preserved lines, protects train movements with a fully operational vintage signaling system. *Brian Solomon*

Above: Robert Fairlie's nineteenth-century twin-firebox articulated locomotive design was intended to provide the equivalent pulling power of a standard gauge locomotive. This narrow gauge locomotive was built in 1992 using the Fairlie patent and was named for David Lloyd George, Britain's prime minister from 1916 to 1922, who was of Welsh heritage. It works on the 13 1/2-mile Festiniog Railway in North Wales. *Brian Solomon*

Opposite top: The Festiniog Railway was a slate-hauling railway with exceptionally narrow tracks, just 1 foot 11 1/2 inches between rails. The line was preserved and today is one of several popular Welsh narrow gauge railways. *Brian Solomon*

Opposite bottom: No. 12 *David Lloyd George* leads a Festiniog train upgrade in the mountains of Wales near Dduallt. This distinctive articulated double-ended locomotive was common on some narrow gauge railways in Britain, Canada, Mexico, and South America. Pioneer American narrow gauge operator the Denver & Rio Grande even ordered one. *Brian Solomon*

179

Above: The Garratt type was built by Beyer Peacock in England and uses an unusual wheel arrangement whereby the whole weight of the locomotive is placed on the driving wheels while its boiler rides on a separate frame suspended between powered sections. This design allows for a relatively powerful locomotive with a big boiler that can operate through very tight curves. *Brian Solomon*

Right: The articulated Garratt was designed by Herbert W. Garratt and built in Manchester by Beyer Peacock for sale to railways around the world. Although never adopted in North America, the type was especially popular in Africa. Some have been used in Britain as well. *Brian Solomon*

North Wales is famous for its 2-foot-gauge railways. In addition to the pioneering Festiniog, numerous other small railways provide excursions using a variety of preserved locomotives. The Welsh Highland Railway at Caernarvon is a 2-foot-gauge line built on portions of an old standard gauge railway and on the alignment of the historic Welsh Highland. This articulated Garrett-type locomotive was built in England for service in South Africa. *Brian Solomon*

After a long day shoveling coal on the footplate, the Irish Rail's Ken Fox looks back over his train from the cab of No. 186 at Farranfore, County Kerry. The Great Southern & Western Railway's 101 class (also known as the J-15 class) 0-6-0 was a jack-of-all-trades and the most common locomotive on Irish railways until displaced by diesels in the 1950s and 1960s. *Brian Solomon*

Above: No. 186 is the oldest serviceable locomotive in Ireland. The design of the 101 class dates to 1867; No. 186 was built in November 1879. Here, it leads an excursion train at Farranfore, County Kerry, in 2006. The Railway Preservation Society of Ireland maintains several steam locomotives for excursion services in the Republic of Ireland and Northern Ireland. *Brian Solomon*

Left: Leading five Cravens-built passenger carriages and a generator van, No. 186 works east near Farranfore in May 2006. In the Victorian period, Ireland was under the yoke of Great Britain, and Irish railways were greatly influenced by their British counterparts. However, where British railways were largely built to Stephenson-standard 4-foot 8-1/2-inch gauge— also standard in the United States—Irish railways are broad gauge, built to 5 feet 3 inches. *Brian Solomon*

Although once the domain of several private companies, by the 1940s, Irish railways were insolvent and the government created a company called Córas Iompair Éireann (Irish Transport Company) to run rail, canal, and highway transport (buses) within the Republic of Ireland. No. 461 was built for the Dublin & South Eastern Railway and is seen here on the old Midland Great Western Railway line at Maynooth during a 1998 Railway Preservation Society of Ireland excursion. *Brian Solomon*

Irish railways remained relatively modest enterprises. Train size did not grow to even the proportions achieved by British counterparts. The largest locomotives were 4-6-0s, and most were substantially smaller. No. 461 was one of two inside-cylinder 2-6-0s built by Beyer Peacock in 1922 for goods (freight) services. It poses on the turntable at Mullingar, County Westmeath, with the Railway Preservation Society of Ireland crew and members of the Irish Rail staff. *Brian Solomon*

Safety valves lift on No. 461 as it waits "in the loop"—what would be called a passing siding in America—at Killucan for the passage of the evening train from Dublin's Connolly Station to Sligo. *Brian Solomon*

Above: Polish National Railways' (PKP) OL49 No. 169 is a heavy 2-6-2 designed for bidirectional running. Large coal reserves and intensive railway activity allowed main-line steam to survive longer in Poland than anywhere else in Europe. The last standard gauge steam roundhouse in regular use in Poland is at Wolsztyn, where privately sponsored locomotive driver (engineer) training has helped keep locomotives in action on regularly scheduled trains. *Brian Solomon*

Opposite top: On May 23, 2000, a PKP Class OL49 2-6-2 works a local freight at Grodzisk Wlkp, Poland. Regular steam-hauled freight services concluded in Poland in 2002, but select passenger trains from Wolsztyn have continued to use steam. *Brian Solomon*

Opposite bottom: Several Polish National Railways Class OL49 2-6-2s have been maintained in serviceable condition in recent years, both for regular passenger services from Wolsztyn and for excursions. In April 28, 2002, No. 111 leads a local train from Wolsztyn to Leszno, Poland. *Brian Solomon*

On a frosty morning at Jenbach, Austria, locomotive No. 4 is under steam and ready for its scheduled run over the narrow gauge Zillertalbahn-to-Mayrhofen. Zillertalbahn is a regional railway that provides regular passenger and freight services using modern diesel-powered equipment, though it operates seasonal steam trains as part of its regular timetable. *Brian Solomon*

Left: No. 4 works in an Alpine setting on its run up to Mayrhofen, Austria. Built by Krauss at Linz, Austria, in 1909, this locomotive worked for years on the Yugoslavian Railways (JZ) as No. JZ-83-076. It is considered a Class 83 and weighs 36 metric tons. *Brian Solomon*

Above: The Zillertalbahn crew prepares No. 4 at Jenbach on an abnormally cold January 2006 morning. This 0-8-2 type was typical of narrow gauge locomotives built for railways of the old Austrian-Hungarian Empire in the early years of the twentieth century. War and politics found the locomotive operating in the newly created Yugoslavia after 1918. *Brian Solomon*

Vintage Diesel
Power

Introduction

Introduction

Dieselization was the most complete and profound change undertaken by American railroading during the mid-twentieth century. To the casual observer, the diesel appears to emerge from the depths of the Depression and bring about an unprecedented motive power revolution in just a few years' time. Most railroads made the transition from steam operations to diesel in a little more than a decade. While there were very few diesels before World War II, during the war they proved their worthiness, and after the war, American railroads embraced rapid large-scale dieselization.

However, diesel *development* was not a sudden process. The success of the diesel locomotive was the result of a blending of internal combustion and electrical technologies made possible by significant technological advances in both areas. American railroads had been familiar with the benefits of electric operations since the first decade of the twentieth century. Electric motors offered better traction characteristics and required far less maintenance than steam power. Electric locomotives enabled greater labor productivity as they made it possible to operate two or more locomotives from a single throttle using multiple-unit connections. The downside of electric locomotives was enormous initial cost of railway electrification.

Parallel with electric railway developments was that of lightweight gasoline-powered railcars colloquially known as doodlebugs. These self-propelled cars were popular in the first decades of the twentieth century for branch-line services. Key to the success of gas-electric cars was matching engine output with the characteristics of the electrical system.

The diesel-electric offered railroads most of the advantages of electric locomotives but without the high cost of electric infrastructure. In the late 1920s and early 1930s, at request of the navy, engine companies embarked on intensive development of compact, lightweight, and mostly high-output diesel engines for marine applications. Key advances to diesel engine design were made possible by the combination of metallurgical improvements, invention of better forms of high-pressure fuel injection, and new manufacturing techniques. Reliable, compact, high-output diesels proved the missing link in the design of powerful diesel-electric locomotives capable of equaling the power potential offered by state-of-the-art steam designs.

During the 1930s, several manufacturers offered diesel switchers. Although experimental road diesels had been tested in the 1920s, the first commercial road-service diesel power was developed by General Motors' Electro-Motive Corporation (later Electro-Motive Division). Following successful production of high-speed power cars for streamliners in the mid-1930s, Electro-Motive developed and perfected the first commercially mass-produced high-horsepower road diesels. This would soon change the face of American railroading. The established locomotive manufacturers, Alco and Baldwin, recognized the potential of Electro-Motive's technology but lagged behind in development and refinement of their own road diesels. Despite the promise of Electro-Motive's diesels, most railroads remained loyal to steam power as they waited to see how the new technology would fare in the harsh environment of railroad road service.

World War II intervened in the development and acceptance of diesel power by imposing complex multifaceted effects on locomotive evolution and application.

The war accelerated the development and refinement process, while temporarily stifling sales of new locomotives and simultaneously pushing railroads and existing locomotive fleets to their practical limits. Wartime traffic proved a high-water mark for traffic moving over American rails. As the war drew to a close, American railroads had a voracious demand for new power. Having experienced the benefits of diesel-electrics during the pressurized wartime traffic environment, railroads were convinced to make the enormous investment in diesel technology.

Although diesel locomotives required higher initial investment, they offered the potential for greater availability, higher reliability, lower maintenance costs, and substantially lower operating costs than steam power. After the war, only a few railroads clung to steam.

Electro-Motive had the advantage in the road-diesel market. After the war, Electro-Motive quickly established its reputation as America's foremost diesel manufacturer. The other builders followed its lead, largely emulating the styles and types of locomotives built by Electro-Motive. Alco and GE initially worked as partners. Railway supplier and diesel engine manufacturer Fairbanks-Morse entered the large locomotive market, viewing diesel locomotives as a logical application for its powerful opposed-piston engine.

Previous pages:
The first decades of American dieselization produced the greatest variety of locomotives. In March 1967 at Central Railroad of New Jersey's Jersey City locomotive terminal, we find CNJ Fairbanks-Morse Train-Master No. 2412, CNJ F-M H-15-44 No. 1502, Reading Company Alco C-430 No. 5211, and Baltimore & Ohio Electro-Motive F7s. Although diesels had ruled for more than a decade, the steam-age coaling tower was still standing. *George W. Kowanski*

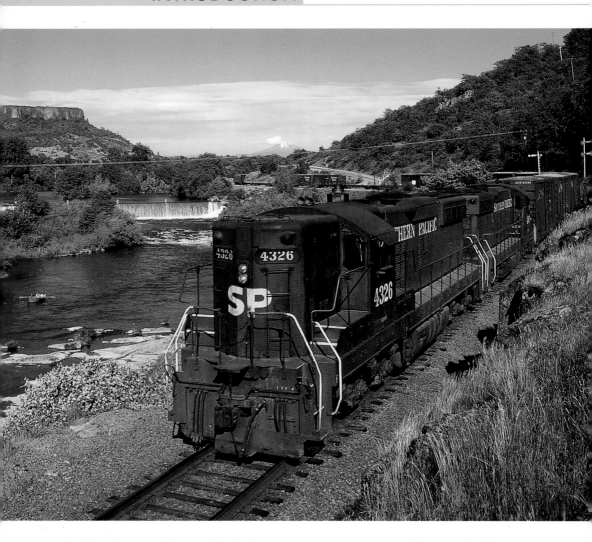

A pair of Southern Pacific SD9s leads the Grants Pass Turn en route from Medford to Grants Pass, Oregon, at Ray Gold on the Siskiyou Line in May 1990. SP's SD9s were known as "Cadillacs" because of the smooth ride afforded by a six-motor Flexicoil truck. For more than three decades, the SD9s were standard power on SP's Oregon branch lines and secondary routes. *Brian Solomon*

In the decade that followed the war, American railroads largely replaced their steam fleets, leading to brisk diesel sales. Electro-Motive grabbed the largest market share. By the mid-1950s, as railroads approached total dieselization, orders began to taper off, which contributed to a shake-out in the industry. Of the big four, Baldwin slipped from third to fourth in the early 1950s and then abandoned locomotive building altogether in 1956. F-M ceased domestic locomotive production in the mid-1950s, although it continued to sell a few locomotives for export into the early 1960s. Alco and GE ended their partnership in 1953, and a few years later GE reentered the market on its own in competition with Electro-Motive and Alco.

By 1960, steam was finished, and railroads looked to start replacing World War II–era diesels with new, more powerful models. Improved designs had substantially increased both output and reliability. The builders sold the concept of two-for-one replacements, and the 3,000- to 3,600-horsepower locomotives offered in the mid-1960s were double the output of the earlier machines.

This book covers the critical three decades of diesel production from the end of World War II (when railroads replaced steam) through the mid-1970s (when railroads replaced the first diesels). It features a variety of models from the five major builders and is intended as a showcase of diesel operations, featuring many different models at work on a number of different lines. While many locomotives are portrayed, the book is not intended as a comprehensive diesel identification guide, nor does it pose to offer a detailed production catalog or complete roster.

The first decades of American dieselization offered unprecedented variety of motive power, and this book features many of the most common models, along with some of the more unusual and obscure types. Photographs were carefully selected to include period images from the steam-to-diesel transition period, along with period views from the 1960s and 1970s, but also more recent images of vintage diesels at work. Among the lasting legacies of some vintage diesel power has been its exceptional durability and longevity. Today, there are operating locomotives that have worked for more than five decades. Yet, some types, notably early road diesels built by Baldwin, were notoriously unreliable and were withdrawn from service after only a few years. Most commercially unsuccessful diesels have been gone for decades. A few rare and unusual diesels have been preserved, but most others are only remembered in photographs.

Chapter 1

Alco

Alco

To better compete for orders with locomotive giant Baldwin Locomotive Works, a host of comparatively small locomotive manufacturers joined together in 1901 to form the American Locomotive Company, long known by the acronym of its initials, Alco. Largest and most significant of Alco's constituent companies was The Schenectady Locomotive Works of Schenectady, New York. In later years this developed as Alco's primary locomotive works in the United States and gradually supplanted the other works that had helped form Alco. To build locomotives for the prosperous Canadian market, Alco acquired the Locomotive and Machine Company of Montreal Limited and changed its name to Montreal Locomotive Works (MLW) in 1908. Both the Schenectady and Montreal facilities manufactured diesel-electrics.

Although primarily a steam builder in it first decades, during the mid-1920s Alco played an important role in the first commercially successful diesel-electric. In 1925, General Electric, Ingersoll-Rand, and Alco formed a diesel-electric construction consortium, wherein Alco supplied mechanical components (primarily the carbodies and running gear). After a few years, Alco left this partnership to develop its own line of diesel switchers. During the late 1920s, Alco acquired a majority share in engine-builder McIntosh & Seymour. Using the M&S engine, Alco introduced a standard end-cab switcher in the early 1930s, and for a few years it was the leader in domestic diesel sales. However, during the 1930s Alco's efforts were eclipsed by Electro-Motive Corporation (known as its Electro-Motive Division after 1940). To better compete with Electro-Motive, in 1940 Alco and GE entered a formal arrangement for the construction and sale of diesel-electric locomotives. By this time, Alco had made formative progress as a builder of road-service diesels.

At request of the War Production Board, Alco focused wartime production on steam designs and diesel switchers. During the crucial years after the war, Alco-GE maintained the number-two position in the domestic locomotive market and sold large numbers of diesels in several key categories.

Its high-speed model PA/PB passenger diesel emulated Electro-Motive's successful E-unit, while the FA/FB road freight diesel was Alco's version of Electro-Motive's groundbreaking F-unit. Significant in Alco's catalog were its road-switcher designs. In 1940, Alco had adapted its S model switcher into a hood unit designed for both switching and roadwork and capable of handling freight or passenger assignments both singly or in multiple. The RS-1 road-switcher set an important precedent soon emulated by the other major diesel builders. After the war, Alco introduced a more powerful road switcher, the model RS-2. In 1950, Alco replaced the RS-2 with its more reliable RS-3, which proved to be one of its bestselling diesels (Louis A. Marre's *Diesel Locomotives: The First 50 Years* lists 366 RS-2s and 1,265 RS-3s sold to U.S. lines). Additional locomotives were built by MLW, and similar types were built and licensed for export.

Although Alco's partnership with GE ended in 1953, it continued to use GE components. Significantly, of the three big steam manufacturers (including Baldwin and Lima), only Alco survived the steam-to-diesel transition. In the mid-1950s, it introduced a new line of diesels based on its recently perfected 251 engine. This line is typified by the RS-11, a rugged 1,800-horsepower four-motor road switcher. The new engine and other technological improvements enabled Alco to survive the first rounds of the "horsepower war" in the late 1950s and 1960s.

In 1963, Alco introduced its improved Century series, as part of its final effort to improve its North American locomotive business. The series featured a variety of refinements that also gave Alco diesels a cleaner exterior design, which many observers consider to be the finest of the era. Century models used an improved designation system logically describing powered axles and horsepower. Each new Alco model used the "C" (for Century) followed by a three-digit number: the first digit indicated powered axles, the second and third represented approximate horsepower.

By this time, Alco was the weakest of the three diesel builders, and despite its best efforts, it ultimately faltered in the high-horsepower market. In 1968, it built its last locomotives, and in early 1969 it exited the U.S. market. In Canada, MLW continued to build locomotives derived from Alco's designs for a few more years.

Previous pages:
Many of Alco's most loyal customers were railroads that operated in the builder's home state of New York. Lehigh Valley bought a variety of Alco diesels, including these RS-11s and C-628s as seen at Sayre, Pennsylvania, on May 31, 1973. Lehigh Valley was one of several bankrupt railroads melded into Conrail on April 1, 1976. *R. R. Richardson photo, Doug Eisele collection*

Switchers needed a short wheelbase to negotiate tight curvature in industrial areas. San Francisco Belt Railroad Alco S-2 No. 25 works street trackage along the Embarcadero on December 14, 1975. In its heyday, the railroad operated 75 miles of industrial and street trackage, largely around San Francisco's waterfront. As the city's industrial base declined, so did the railroad. The Belt no longer moves freight; today new tracks along the city's Embarcadero carry electric streetcars for the Municipal Railway. *Brian Jennison*

Massachusetts' Grafton & Upton Railroad is among the most unusual lines in the state. It began as a narrow gauge line, was later converted to standard gauge, then was electrified as an interurban, and today survives as a short-line freight carrier. In February 1963, a G&U Alco S-2 working cab-first moves freight at Grafton. *Jim Shaughnessy*

In the mid-1980s, Connecticut's K&L Feeds acquired former Central Vermont Railway Alco S-4 No. 8081. The freshly painted switcher reposes in the morning sun at CV's New London Yard on February 28, 1988. Today the locomotive is preserved at the Connecticut Eastern Railroad Museum in Willimantic. *Brian Solomon*

A view of the short hood on Genesee & Wyoming RS-1 No. 25 at Retsof, New York. This 1,000-horsepower Alco-GE road switcher was built for G&W in 1952. It was photographed 35 years later at Retsof, where it was still working for the same railroad. *Brian Solomon*

This detail shows the short hood and headlight on G&W RS-1 No. 1976. Built by Alco in May 1955 as G&W No. 30, the locomotive was renamed *E. P. McCloskey*, renumbered, and painted red, white, and blue for the American bicentennial. *Brian Solomon*

New York, Susquehanna & Western was among the earliest railroads to fully dieselize regular operations. By the end of World War II, it largely relied on Alco switchers and road switchers. On August 7, 1959, NYS&W RS-1 No. 231 was at Erie Railroad's Jersey City Terminal with a passenger train destined for Butler, New Jersey. *Richard Jay Solomon*

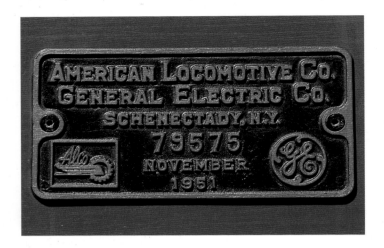

Rutland Railroad Alco RS-1 No. 405 was built by Alco-GE at Schenectady, New York, in November 1951. Less than two years later, GE dissolved its locomotive-building partnership with Alco, although it continued to supply Alco with primary electrical components. After its split with GE, Alco redesigned its locomotive line and introduced a new diesel prime mover. *Brian Solomon*

Green Mountain, now a component of the Vermont Rail System, is one of the last regular users of an Alco RS-1 road switcher and routinely assigns former Rutland Railroad No. 405 to passenger excursion service on old home rails. *Brian Solomon*

Green Mountain Railroad No. 405 leads an excursion on the old Rutland Railroad at Proctorville, Vermont, on October 9, 2004. Typically excursions operate between Bellows Falls and Chester, but on this day the route was extended beyond its normal limits to Proctorsville. Here the excursion met the daily freight from Rutland, Vermont, much to the excitement of local residents. *Brian Solomon*

Above: The versatility of the RS-1 allowed it to work a great variety of trains. Chicago & Western Indiana was one of Chicago's most obscure passenger carriers. In June 1961, C&WI Alco RS-1 No. 259 leads a short train near 16th Street. On the upper level a group of Rock Island Alco road switchers await duty for the evening suburban rush hour from LaSalle Street Station. *Richard Jay Solomon*

Opposite top: In January 1969, Vermont Railway RS-1s 404 and 402 lead a freight on the former Rutland Railroad between Emerald Lake and East Dorset, Vermont. Vermont Railway 404 was built for Duluth, South Shore & Atlantic in 1946 and acquired by Vermont Railway in 1967 to add to its fleet of former Rutland Railroad RS-1s. *Jim Shaughnessy*

Opposite bottom: The RS-1 was equally at home on the main line, out on a branch, or working in the yard. On August 19, 1972, Penn Central RS-1 No. 9910 was caught at the east end of Goodman Street Yard in Rochester, New York, on the famed former New York Central Water Level Route. Penn Central inherited RS-1s from all three of its constituent railroads. *R. R. Richardson photo, Doug Eisele collection*

New York Central painted RS-3 No. 8223 at Conrail's DeWitt Yard. Central had been one of Alco's best customers in steam days and continued to order large numbers of Alco products into the diesel era. While Central also placed substantial orders with Alco's competitors, it remained loyal to Alco right through the late 1960s. *Brian Solomon*

Left: This detail shows the short hood on New York Central No. 8223 wearing the classic lightning stripe livery. In their day, Central's legions of Alco road switchers were hardly worth a passing glance; today this preserved locomotive is viewed as a gem from the early days of dieselization. *Brian Solomon*

Below: New York Central No. 8223 as seen from the cab of an F-unit on the Adirondack Scenic Railroad at Thendera, New York, on July 22, 2004. Along with Electro-Motive's F-unit, the Alco RS-3 was among the most common locomotives built during the steam-to-diesel transition period. Adirondack Scenic Railroad uses a variety of vintage diesels to offer passenger excursions of former New York Central lines in upstate New York. *Brian Solomon*

On Providence & Worcester's first day of independent operation in 1973, a leased Delaware & Hudson RS-3 gleams in fresh P&W paint outside the Worcester engine house. Once a component of New Haven Railroad, P&W sought independence after New Haven's inclusion in the doomed Penn Central merger of the late 1960s. *Jim Shaughnessy*

Penn Central and Conrail repowered a number of RS-3s using EMD 567 engines salvaged from scrapped E-units. The repowered locomotives were designated RS-3M and operated in secondary service. On June 10, 1982, Conrail RS-3M No. 9905 leads the wire train on the old New Haven Railroad at Mount Vernon, New York. George W. Kowanski was the engineer that day and took the opportunity to make this rare photograph. *George W. Kowanski*

New Haven RS-3s rest in front of the Waterbury, Connecticut, railway station in June 1960. Today New Haven RS-3 No. 529 is preserved in operating condition on the Naugatuck Railroad, which operates through its namesake valley to the north of Waterbury. *Richard Jay Solomon*

Road switchers by nature were versatile machines suited to a variety of assignments. Rock Island was one of many railroads that assigned them to suburban service, where their rapid loading characteristics allowed them to maintain tight schedules. In July 1958, Rock Island No. 497 works a Chicago–Blue Island train. *Richard Jay Solomon*

Lehigh Valley Alco RS-3 No. 215 drills the yard at Manchester, New York, on October 17, 1971. Alcos were famous for their smoke shows when notched out rapidly; the 244 engine in particular was especially smoky. *R. R. Richardson photo, Doug Eisele collection*

Opposite bottom: Western Maryland had four RS-3s equipped with both dynamic brakes and steam generators, options which when combined mandated a high short hood. Only five RS-3s were built this way; the fifth went to the Pennsylvania Railroad and later was traded to the Lehigh Valley, becoming its No. 211. On May 13, 1972, a pair of WM FAs leads RS-3 No. 192 and an Electro-Motive F-unit at Hagerstown. In the 1950s, WM pioneered multiple-unit connections between Alco and Electro-Motive locomotives. *R. R. Richardson photo, Doug Eisele collection*

Freshly painted Battenkill Railroad RS-3 No. 605 is seen at Eagle Bridge, New York, on May 13, 1984. Formerly Vermont Railway No. 605, it has served Battenkill Railroad in the same paint livery for 25 years—longer than many other RS-3s worked American rails. *Jim Shaughnessy*

On October 20, 2009, Battenkill Railroad RS-3 No. 605 has just passed Shushan, New York, on its run to Eagle Bridge, where the railroad interchanges freight with CP Rail and Pan Am Southern's Boston & Maine route. The Battenkill operates a few miles of former Delaware & Hudson secondary lines in eastern New York State. *Brian Solomon*

A detail of the short hood on No. 605 shows the classic Hancock air whistle and twin sealed-beam headlight. In 2010, this was among the last as-built RS-3s in revenue freight service in North America. More than 1,750 RS-2s and RS-3s were built, but today only a handful survives outside of museums. *Brian Solomon*

A quartet of Alco FA/FBs leading an eastward freight on the Boston & Albany approaches the west portal of State Line Tunnel near Canaan, New York. New York Central operated the largest fleet of Alco FA/FB cab units. *Jim Shaughnessy*

New York Central's Alco FA-2 freight diesels rest between assignments at the former West Shore yards in North Bergen, New Jersey, on April 13, 1958. Alco's FA/FB was a carbody type that emulated Electro-Motive's successful F-unit. Central routinely operated FA/FBs in multiple for more than two decades, although in later years it was common to find them mixed with other models. *Richard Jay Solomon*

In the late 1940s, a nearly new A-B-A set of Alco FA diesels exits the east portal of State Line Tunnel with an eastward freight. In 1947, Alco diesels began supplanting Boston & Albany's famous Lima-built Berkshire-type steam locomotives on road freights. By 1951, the road was fully dieselized, making it the first major component of the New York Central system to be operated entirely with diesels. *Robert A. Buck*

Erie Lackawanna FA-1 No. 7254 catches the sun east of Buffalo at Bison Yard in Sloan, New York, in July 1968. EL inherited its FA/FBs from the Erie Railroad. Powered by Alco's 244 engine, the FA-1 was rated at 1,500 horsepower. While many railroads used FA models into the 1960s, these Alco road units were not as well regarded as the EMD F-units and had become rare by 1970. *Doug Eisele collection*

An A-B-A set of Baltimore & Ohio Alco FAs wearing the as-delivered two-tone blue leads a westward freight at Creston in east-central Ohio in the mid-1950s. B&O operated a moderate-sized fleet of Alco FA/FB-2s built between 1950 and 1953. Rated at 1,600 horsepower, these were nominally more powerful than Electro-Motive's F7, which was a more common type on B&O lines in the 1950s. *J. William Vigrass*

In the early 1960s, just a few years after the fateful merger between Erie Railroad and one-time competitor Delaware, Lackawanna & Western, Erie-Lackawanna FA-1 No. 7321 rolls across a weed-grown diamond crossing near Campbell Hall, New York. Erie Railroad connected with the New Haven at nearby Maybrook, New York, not far from Campbell Hall. This served as gateway to New England, which resulted in considerable freight interchange between the two lines. *Richard Jay Solomon*

A Southern Pacific Alco PA cab leads the *Shasta Daylight* at Dunsmuir, California, in 1961. The Alco PA employed a single turbocharged 244 engine, which was four-cycle diesel introduced in 1944 to generate 2,000 horsepower. The later PA-2/PB-2s were even more powerful and rated at 2,250 horsepower. Greater output, more rugged traction motors, and dynamic braking were among the reasons that SP favored the PA for passenger services on heavily graded routes. *Bob Morris*

An Alco PA and EMD F7A work upgrade in the Colorado Front Range with Rio Grande's *Yampa Valley Mail* in 1963. Although PAs and Fs would have rarely worked together on most railroads, such combinations were not uncommon on the Rio Grande. *Jim Shaughnessy*

In 1961, Santa Fe Railway PA No. 75 leads the eastward *San Francisco Chief* across the Western Pacific crossing at Stockton, California. Santa Fe was among the last original buyers to operate PAs in passenger service. In the late 1960s, Delaware & Hudson acquired four Santa Fe PAs, and today two of these are preserved. *Bob Morris*

Just after 11:00 a.m. on July 16, 1958, warbonnet-painted Alco PAs lead Santa Fe train No. 13 west from Chicago's Dearborn Station. The first Alco PA was symbolically assigned Alco's 75,000 builder number and after tests on Lehigh Valley was sold to Santa Fe, becoming its No. 51. *Richard Jay Solomon*

In 1961, a year after the Erie-Lackawanna merger, an Alco PA in full Erie paint idles at Lackawanna's Hoboken Terminal on the Jersey side of the Hudson opposite Manhattan. On the left is a set of Lackawanna F3s, and looming through the smog is the famous Empire State Building. Among the consolidations facilitated by the merger was Erie abandoning its Jersey City terminal in favor of Lackawanna's Hoboken Terminal. *Richard Jay Solomon*

On May 10, 1959, Lehigh Valley Alco PA diesels are exchanged for a Pennsylvania Railroad GG1 electric near Newark, New Jersey. Lehigh Valley passenger trains served Pennsy's Penn Station in New York City, which required the change of locomotives because diesels are not allowed in the tunnels beneath the Hudson River. Once famous for its *Black Diamond*, Lehigh Valley ended all passenger service in 1961. *Richard Jay Solomon*

Three of D&H's former Santa Fe Alco PAs are seen inside Colonie Shops in October 1973. D&H was the last railroad in the United States to operate classic PA diesels. D&H sent its PAs to Morrison-Knudsen for rebuilding in the late 1970s and then leased them to Boston's Massachusetts Bay Transportation Authority for a stint in suburban service before selling them to a New Jersey–based leasing company that shipped them to Mexico. *Jim Shaughnessy*

D&H bought secondhand PA diesels for passenger service. However, after the advent of Amtrak in 1971 temporarily left D&H without a passenger train, it assigned PAs to freight work. Later, when passenger services were restored between Albany and Montreal, the PAs were rebuilt and put back to work as intended. This rare photograph shows all four PAs on D&H's southward SC-1 local freight running along the shore of Lake Champlain at Port Henry, New York. *Jim Shaughnessy*

Three Delaware & Hudson PAs lead the southward *Susquehanna Valley Special* excursion on the Albany main south of Albany, New York, on September 29, 1973. Although D&H was one of the best known operators of PAs, the railroad was one of the few operators that had not bought them new from Alco. *Brian Jennison*

New York, Chicago & St. Louis Railroad was a mouthful, so the line was better known as the Nickel Plate Road—abbreviated as NKP. A pair of NKP PA diesels arrives at Buffalo with an eastward passenger train. Nickel Plate's were among the most attractively painted Alco passenger locomotives. Built by Alco-GE in 1947 and 1948, Nickel Plate Road's PAs were all rated at 2,000 horsepower. *Jay Williams collection*

In 1947, Pennsylvania Railroad bought 10 PAs and 5 cab-less PB "boosters" from Alco. These had been intended for passenger service, but within a decade the Pennsy reassigned them to less glamorous jobs. On May 4, 1957, Nos. 5751A and 5757A work as helpers along with a venerable I1s Decapod on freight climbing northward on the Elmira Branch. *Jim Shaughnessy*

In March 1958, NKP Alco PA No. 183 leads No. 7 westbound at Cleggville, Cleveland, Ohio. In 1962, NKP traded its PA fleet back to Alco on an order for RS-36 road switchers. *W. McCaleb photo, Jay Williams collection*

Falls Road Railroad Alco RS-11 No. 1802 is a former Nickel Plate Road locomotive and one of several RS-11s operated by parent company Genesee Valley Transportation. The RS-11 is powered by a 1,800-horsepower 251 diesel engine. *Brian Solomon*

On July 17, 2006, Falls Road Railroad Alco RS-11 No. 1802 works its way east with a local freight on the former New York Central Falls Road from Lockport to Brockport. Back in New York Central times this was Alco territory, and today it is again. *Brian Solomon*

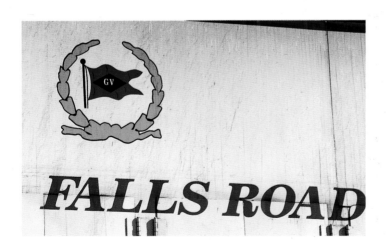

New York Central's Falls Road provided a direct route from Rochester to Niagara Falls, New York, and served through freight and passenger trains. Today it is just a dead-end branch used for local freight traffic. *Brian Solomon*

In July 1963, a new New York Central RS-32 leads an eastward freight down the Hudson Division toward New York City. Central bought the 2,000-horsepower RS-32 for use in fast freight service. This was a relatively unusual type; the only other railroad to buy the model new was Southern Pacific. *Richard Jay Solomon*

Today, Genesee Valley Transportation's Falls Road Railroad short line routinely assigns former New York Central RS-32 No. 2035 to local work on the old New York Central Falls Road route. On October 13, 2008, engineer Russ Young switches sidings serving a new ethanol plant on the line. *Brian Solomon*

A close-up shows the Genesee Valley Transportation nose decal on Falls Road Railroad No. 2035, working its namesake branch. Among the characteristics of the classic vintage RS-32 is the long one-piece front windshield that spans the width of the nose section. All RS-32s were built with low short hoods to give the crew better forward visibility. *Brian Solomon*

Lehigh Valley C-420 No. 415 is seen in Cornell Red at Sayre, Pennsylvania, on March 14, 1976. In less than a month, Lehigh Valley would be absorbed by Conrail, and this C-420 would be one of 12 conveyed to Delaware & Hudson. D&H was expanded as a part of the federally sponsored creation of Conrail in order to provide the guise of rail competition over selected Conrail routes. *Bill Dechau photo, Doug Eisele collection*

Lehigh Valley C-420 No. 406 works an eastward freight through Odessa, New York. The C-420 was built in both low short hood and high hood variations. Lehigh Valley, Lehigh & Hudson River, Monon, Long Island, and Louisville & Nashville were among the railroads to order this attractively designed road switcher. *R. R. Richardson photo, Doug Eisele collection*

On October 5, 1974, Lehigh Valley No. 415 and two other LV C-420s lead an eastward freight. All are in Lehigh's as-delivered gray and yellow livery. With the introduction of the Century series in 1963, the C-420 was the 2,000-horsepower model that succeeded the short-lived RS-32. Where only 35 RS-32s were built, the C-420 accounted for 131 units, including a pair sold to Mexico. *R. R. Richardson photo, Doug Eisele collection*

Left and below: Maine Eastern runs trains on the former Maine Central Rockland Branch east from Brunswick to its namesake. Among its freight operations is the short haul from Dragon Cement in Thomaston to shipping barges at Rockland. In August 2004, New Jersey's Morristown & Erie—operator of Maine Eastern—provided power for the cement train in the form of a former CP Rail C-424. The three-car train of pressurized cement hoppers is seen on its way through Rockland on the way to the docks. *Both photos Brian Solomon*

Opposite: CP Rail C-424 No. 4206 catches the sun at Guelph Junction, Ontario, on September 24, 1988. This Montreal-built locomotive was very similar to its Schenectady-built counterparts. Alco's longtime Canadian affiliate Montreal Locomotive Works not only built Alco-designed locomotives for the Canadian market, but it continued to build locomotives for several years after Alco ended domestic production in 1969. *Brian Solomon*

Genesee Valley Transportation's Delaware-Lackawanna operates a network of former Delaware, Lackawanna & Western and Delaware & Hudson lines radiating from Scranton, Pennsylvania. In September 1996, D-L C-425 No. 2452 works the old D&H main line south of downtown Scranton. One of several former Erie-Lackawanna Alcos operated by D-L, No. 2452 wears a livery similar to that of the old E-L. *Brian Solomon*

Above: Former Erie-Lackawanna C-425 No. 2461 leads Delaware-Lackawanna's PT98 working west toward Scranton on the former DL&W main line on its return trip from Slateford Junction. In its heyday, this was a busy triple-track main line serving as a corridor for coal and manifest freight as well as express passenger trains. *Brian Solomon*

Left: In the 1960s, Erie-Lackawanna urged Alco to boost output of its C-424 to 2,500 horsepower to match General Electric's U25B. E-L ordered a dozen of the new C-425s. Today, short-line operator Genesee Valley Transportation operates several former E-L C-425s on its lines in New York and Pennsylvania. Old E-L No. 2461 catches the morning sun at Scranton just a short distance from the old Delaware, Lackawanna & Western shops. *Brian Solomon*

A short portion of the old Delaware, Lackawanna & Western main line in western New York State is run by Bath & Hammondport. On May 9, 2007, a pair of C-424Ms lead B&H's freight toward Painted Post, New York, on the line that once hosted famous named passenger trains, such as the *Lackawanna Limited* and the streamlined *Phoebe Snow*. *Brian Solomon*

B&H C-424M No. 422 leads a freight working the former DL&W main line near Savona, New York, on May 9, 2007. Among the perceived advantages of the Erie-Lackawanna merger was the ability to consolidate redundant facilities and parallel routes. Erie-Lackawanna favored former Erie Railroad routes west of Binghamton; as a result much of the old DL&W was downgraded. This segment of old DL&W main line now serves as a short-line branch, where as late as 1964 it carried through freight and passenger trains to Buffalo. *Brian Solomon*

Built by Alco in 1963 as Erie-Lackawanna No. 2414, B&H C-424M No. 422 has had a long history. In the 1970s, it was acquired by Delaware & Hudson (No. 451), which had the locomotive rebuilt as a C-424M, lowering output from 2,400 to 2,000 horsepower. Today, it is back on old home rails working for B&H, one of several short lines affiliated with Livonia, Avon & Lakeville that operate segments of former E-L trackage. *Brian Solomon*

A cab detail of Western New York & Pennsylvania No. 430 shows the distinctive angled windshield, contoured cab roof, and classification lights that are unique to Alco's Century series. Introduced in 1967 to compete with Electro-Motive's GP40, the 3,000-horsepower C-430 was the most powerful of Alco's four-motor Centuries. No. 430 was originally New York Central No. 2050 and later served Penn Central, Conrail, and New York, Susquehanna & Western. *Brian Solomon*

On July 19, 2009, WNY&P No. 430 leads two other Centuries with the westward HNME (Hornell, New York, to Meadville, Pennsylvania) near Andover, New York, on the former Erie Railroad main line. In the early 1990s, Conrail discontinued operations on the former Erie west of Hornell, yet a decade later the line was revived and reopened by WNY&P. *Brian Solomon*

WNY&P is a short line affiliated with Livonia, Avon & Lakeville that operates on portions of the old Erie Railroad and Pennsylvania Railroad using an eclectic fleet of Alco and Montreal Locomotive Works diesels. WNY&P Alco C-430 No. 430 is seen at Allegany Yard, in Olean, New York, on October 11, 2008. *Brian Solomon*

Lehigh Valley Alco C-628s lead a westward freight under the Hamilton Street bridge in Allentown, Pennsylvania, in February 1975. After Lehigh Valley was melded into the federally planned Conrail system in 1976, its six-motor Alcos were reassigned to other routes. Most finished up their service in the late 1970s working mineral trains on the former Pennsylvania Railroad out of Mingo Junction, Ohio. *George W. Kowanski*

In late winter sun in early March 1973 at Crescent, New York, a quartet of Lehigh Valley Alco C-628s work eastward on a Delaware & Hudson/Lehigh Valley pool freight destined for Mechanicville, New York. Lehigh Valley ultimately acquired 17 C-628s, including 9 former Monon units. *Jim Shaughnessy*

Lehigh Valley C-628 No. 636 rests with another Century on the ready tracks near the railroad's steam-era shop complex at Sayre, Pennsylvania, on May 24, 1972. No. 636 was former Monon No. 404, one of nine units the Midwestern line traded back to Alco after just a few years in service. *R. R. Richardson photo, Doug Eisele collection*

In May 1965, three new Alco C-628s deliver 8,250 horsepower on a southward Delaware & Hudson freight reaching the crest of Richmondville Hill. For a very short time, Alco's 2,750-horsepower C-628 was the most powerful single-engine single-unit diesel-electric on the commercial market in North America. More powerful "double diesels" were bought by Union Pacific and Southern Pacific using pairs of prime movers. *Jim Shaughnessy*

Monon bought nine Alco C-628s, which it intended to use in unit coal train service. When the coal contract fizzled, the railroad operated the units in regular freight service before trading them back to Alco on an order for less powerful but more versatile C-420s. Monon No. 408 was photographed at Bloomington, Indiana, in November 1965. *Jay Williams collection*

In May 1968, new Alco C-628s sit outside Alco's Schenectady Works awaiting shipment to Nacionales de Mexico. In less than a year, Alco would cease locomotive production, ending a long history of continuous locomotive construction at this site. N. de M. bought 32 C-628s from Alco and was one of three railroads to work these locomotives south of the border. *Jim Shaughnessy*

On July 24, 1997, Cape Breton & Central Nova Scotia freight No. 305 works westward with M-630 No. 2034 climbing the 1.5 percent grade to Marshy Hope, Nova Scotia. CB&CNS operated 245 miles of trackage spun off from Canadian National Railways in 1993. Initially the railroad used a mix of secondhand Alco-designed diesels built by affiliate Montreal Locomotive Works to move its freight trains. *Brian Solomon*

Cape Breton & Central Nova Scotia M-630 catches the setting sun at Afton, Nova Scotia, on July 25, 1997. CB&CNS continued to operate six-motor MLWs in road service in Canada for a few years after Canadian National and CP Rail had disposed of their big Century fleets. *Brian Solomon*

Cape Breton & Central Nova Scotia's insignia on the side of an M-630. Although Alco ended locomotive production at its Schenectady, New York, plant, MLW continued to build diesels to Alco designs for a few more years. *Brian Solomon*

On the evening of July 25, 1997, a trio of Cape Breton & Central Nova Scotia M-630s labor on the climb to Marshy Hope. Alcos were known for their great pulling power at slow speeds, but on this day the grade got the better of the locomotives and the crew needed to "double the hill" (take the tonnage up in two trips). *Brian Solomon*

By the mid-1990s, six-motor Alco locomotives were an anachronism, thus giving the remote CB&CNS an antique mystique. M-630 No. 2034, named *Sir Conan Doyle,* leads westward freight 305. *Brian Solomon*

Just after noontime on July 26, 1997, CB&CNS M-630 No. 2003 rolls past the general store in Merigomish, Nova Scotia. The days of the six-motor Alco working heavy freight on CB&CNS were short-lived; after a few years the railroad replaced them with less colorful diesels. *Brian Solomon*

The isolated 260-mile Cartier Railway between Port Cartier and Mont Wright was built in the 1950s to tap enormous iron ore reserves in northeastern Quebec. Three M-636s/C-636s with an empty ore train growl upgrade through wilderness in the Sept-Îles National Park many miles north of Port Cartier. *Brian Solomon*

Loaded ore trains on the Cartier are not allowed great speed, yet this panned shot of Cartier No. 82 from July 12, 1997, makes it appear as if the big Century is really moving. An order for six-motor General Electric diesels in 2001 ended Alco/MLW supremacy on this isolated line. *Brian Solomon*

Three C-636/M-636s led by Cartier No. 82 bring a heavy ore train south of Dog siding in Quebec's Sept-Îles National Park. The remoteness and wonderful scenery of this line are great attractions for photographers. *Brian Solomon*

Western New York & Pennsylvania has acquired several former Cartier six-motor Alco/MLW diesels for work on its lines radiating out of Olean, New York. On October 12, 2008, WNY&P No. 637 works the westward HNME (Hornell, New York, to Meadville, Pennsylvania) on the old Erie Railroad main line near Cambridge Springs, Pennsylvania. *Brian Solomon*

In the 1960s, Erie-Lackawanna routinely dispatched Alco Centuries on long freight trains making their way to Midwestern gateways. Four decades later, old Alco diesels ply the line with local freight. On October 8, 2009, the sounds of Alco 251 engines permeate the morning mist as WNY&P's HNME works west of Union City, Pennsylvania, with M-636 No. 637 in the lead. *Brian Solomon*

WNY&P M-636 No. 637 rolls through Saegertown on the last lap of its run from Hornell, New York, to Meadville, Pennsylvania, over the former Erie Railroad main line. *Brian Solomon*

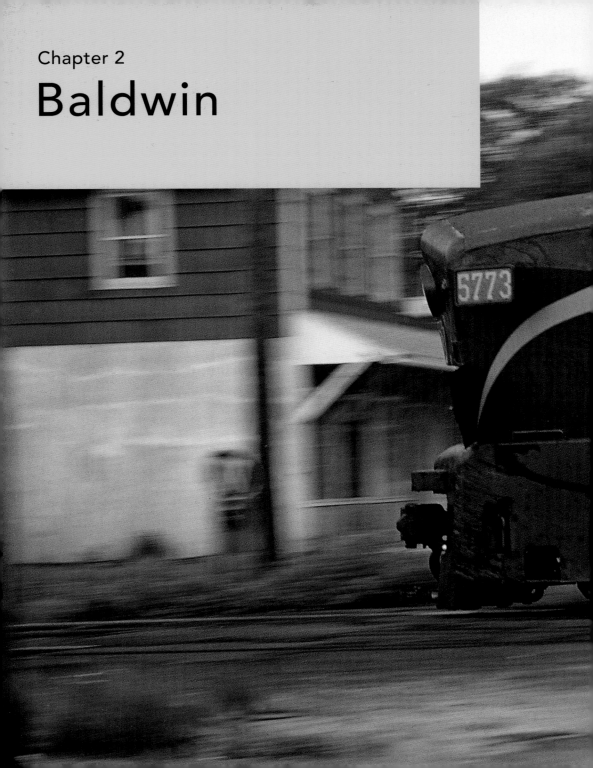

Chapter 2
Baldwin

Baldwin

ounded by Matthias W. Baldwin, the Baldwin Locomotive Works began building steam locomotives in 1831 and at the dawn of the diesel age was America's oldest surviving locomotive manufacturer. Although it was a master of steam locomotive construction and early to anticipate the practicality of the diesel, Baldwin delayed in developing commercial diesel-electric technology. However, in 1931, Baldwin acquired established engine manufacturers I. P. Morris and De La Vergne and transferred production to its Eddystone, Pennsylvania, plant with the aim of developing a diesel locomotive engine. Eddystone was a relatively modern plant, having been completed in the 1920s as a spacious replacement for Baldwin's old facilities in downtown Philadelphia. Initially, Baldwin constructed its diesels in the steam locomotive tender shop, because the diesel bodies were similar in construction to tenders.

Baldwin's first commercial diesels, and by far its greatest success in the diesel market, were switchers it introduced in the late 1930s and improved after World War II. It built approximately 1,900 diesel

switchers during its two decades in the diesel business, offering models in the 660- to 800- and 1,000- to 1,200-horsepower range. Of these, the 1,000-horsepower types were the most common.

During the war, Baldwin's efforts to develop high-horsepower road diesels were unsuccessful; after the war, it continued to build some respectable road switchers, but its postwar approach to road diesels yielded eclectic and curious designs that compared poorly with those of its competition. Most lasted only a few years in service before requiring rebuilding, often with Electro-Motive engines.

In 1950, Baldwin merged with Lima-Hamilton. Lima had been the smallest of the "big three" commercial steam locomotive manufacturers. It was only in the diesel business for about two years following the acquisition. Although the company retained the Lima name and was known afterward as Baldwin-Lima-Hamilton, it discontinued Lima's diesel line in favor of the more successful Baldwin diesels. Despite improvements to its locomotives, Baldwin found it increasingly difficult to compete and exited commercial locomotive manufacturing in 1956. Its switchers proved the longest lived; as late as 2010, a few survive in freight service on North American short lines. Although bought by a variety of railroads, Baldwin's road locomotives were few in number compared with the vast quantities of Alco and Electro-Motive products used to dieselize the railroads following World War II.

Compared with Alco and Electro-Motive, Baldwin's total diesel production was relatively small, yet between 1937 and 1956 it constructed roughly three dozen different diesel models for domestic applications. Baldwin's variety, combined with its relative obscurity, has long made its diesels fascinating to locomotive enthusiasts. Many Baldwin models were unique to specific railroads. For example, Pennsylvania Railroad was the only line to buy the DR-6-4-2000 with the "shark-nose" body style. Other lines bought similar DR-6-4-2000s that featured the "baby-face" body style. With Baldwin, however, looks can be deceiving, as different body styles were used on models with nearly identical specifications. Furthermore, in some situations, entirely different models had similar body styles. For example, no less than three domestic models were built using the shark-nose body, yet one of these models, the DR-4-4-15, was also built with the baby-face design.

Baldwin used a different system for operating locomotives in multiple than other builders. For this reason, Baldwin diesels tended not to work with other builders' diesels. Some railroads, such as New York Central, later rebuilt Baldwins, increasing their operating life and making them more versatile.

Baldwin's diesels had a distinctive sound to them as well. The De La Vergne diesel was a four-cycle design that Baldwin built in various configurations using both normally aspirated and turbocharged designs. It had maximum rotational speed of 625 rpm (much slower than the engines of other builders) and made a ponderous sound at lower throttle positions while producing a thrashing at full throttle.

Baldwin was a pioneer of the six-motor diesel-electric, which were among the company's best diesel products. These were designed for high-tractive effort applications and known for their ability to haul heavy tonnage at slow speeds for extended periods. A few railroads bought Baldwins for passenger service, but these locomotives tended to fair poorly and were typically reassigned to freight work after just a few years. As a result, photographs of Baldwin diesels hauling passenger trains are relatively rare.

Previous pages:
Using a slow shutter speed and Kodachrome film, Richard Jay Solomon made this pan image of a Pennsy DR-6-4-2000 shark nose in the spring of 1964. Pennsylvania Railroad operated a unique fleet of six-axle Baldwin passenger sharks riding on A1A trucks (center axle unpowered). Pennsy initially assigned these to premier *Limited* trains west of Harrisburg. In later years, they were relegated to commuter work on the New York & Long Branch between Bay Head Junction, South Amboy, and Jersey City, New Jersey. *Richard Jay Solomon*

Oakland Terminal Baldwin DS-4-4-1000 No. 101 works yard trackage off Wood Street in Oakland, California, on November 4, 1980. OT bought the locomotive new in 1948. Now owned by the Pacific Locomotive Association and stored in Niles Canyon at Brightside, California, it is one of several preserved Baldwin diesels in the United States. *Brian Jennison*

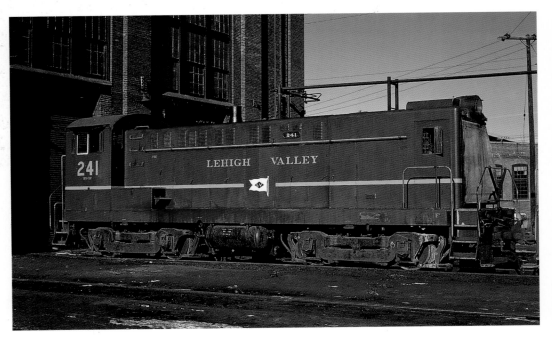

Many railroads got their first taste for Baldwin switchers during World War II, when Baldwin was limited to the production of diesel switchers and steam locomotives. Lehigh Valley bought five VO1000-type switchers in 1944. Nearly 30 years later, on February 13, 1973, LV No. 241—a Baldwin-Lima-Hamilton S-12 from 1950—rests at the company shops in Sayre, Pennsylvania. *Doug Eisele*

Sierra Railroad S-12 No. 44 works east of Oakdale, California, at Cooperstown on April 3, 1993. Although Sierra bought some of its Baldwin diesels new, this locomotive came secondhand from Sharon Steel. Sierra is one of a few railroads that continue to operate Baldwins in freight service decades after Baldwin exited the business. *Brian Solomon*

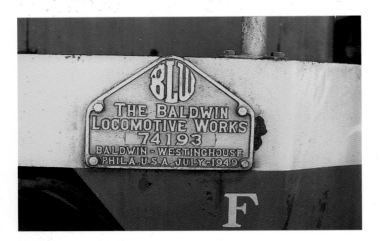

California Western DS-4-4-1000 switcher No. 53 was built new for the U.S. government in July 1949. Many California short lines acquired Baldwin diesels in the 1940s and 1950s and continued to operate them decades after Baldwin ended locomotive production and after larger railroads replaced Baldwins with EMD products. *Brian Jennison*

California Western RS-12 No. 56 leads Stillwell passenger cars on an excursion between Willits and Fort Bragg on July 1, 1976. The railroad's gas cars are known as "Skunk Trains"; when these prove inadequate to handle passenger loads, locomotive-hauled Super Skunks take over. *Brian Jennison*

California Western RS-12 No. 56 leads a "Super Skunk" excursion between Willits and Fort Bragg on July 13, 1985. Baldwin's RS-12 was a 1,200-horsepower road switcher designed for light road work and was well suited to short-line and branch-line operation. *Brian Jennison*

Although standard today, in the 1950s six-motor diesels were an operational anomaly. On July 28, 1958, a pair of Chesapeake & Ohio's Baldwin-built AS-616s grinds past the tower at Covington, Kentucky, with a long cut of coal hoppers. The AS-616 was among Baldwin's more successful efforts and was generally well regarded for heavy slow-speed work. The AS-616 was the successor to Baldwin's DRS-6-6-1500 and was nominally more powerful (rated at 1,600 horsepower to the older model's 1,500 horsepower). *Richard Jay Solomon*

Baldwin's heavy road switcher was powered with the 608SC engine and was initially rated at 1,500 horsepower. It was offered to railroads as a four-motor with either B-B or A1A trucks, or as a six-motor with C-C trucks. These types were respectively designated as models DRS-4-4-1500, DRS-6-4-1500, and DRS-6-6-1500. Erie-Lackawanna DRS-6-6-1500 No. 1156 was photographed at Buffalo, New York, on October 4, 1970. *Doug Eisele*

Ore-hauling Bessemer & Lake Erie operated an eclectic fleet of six-motor diesels a generation before six-motor types were standard power on other freight-hauling lines. B&LE's DRS-6-6-1500 No. 403 works at Albion, Pennsylvania, on June 7, 1970. It emerged from Baldwin's Eddystone plant 20 years earlier and enjoyed a relatively long career hauling heavy tonnage. *Doug Eisele*

In 1974, D&H acquired the last active pair of shark-nose diesels from a Pennsylvania-based scrap dealer. Originally New York Central locomotives, these had been among nine RF-16s that worked on the Pennsylvania mineral-hauling Monongahela Railway. They are pictured at Mechanicville shortly after their arrival on D&H property. *Jim Shaughnessy*

Delaware & Hudson RF-16 No. 1216 is shown at Mechanicville, New York, on February 15, 1975. By the time D&H acquired these "sharks," the type was all but extinct elsewhere. D&H operated them for just a few years before selling them to a short line. Although they have not operated in many years, both surviving sharks remain extant. *Jim Shaughnessy*

Baldwin's RF-16s were designed and geared for freight service, making passenger excursions such as this one a rare occurrence. On September 20, 1975, D&H's famous pair of former New York Central RF-16s leads an excursion destined for Whitehall and the rarely traveled Washington Branch. *Jim Shaughnessy*

Pennsylvania Railroad RF-16 No. 9595 rests at Cleveland's Kinsman Yard on July 11, 1958. The Pennsy, like many owners of Baldwin road diesels, tended to assign them to very heavy freights; Pennsy, New York Central, and Baltimore & Ohio all operated shark-nose models in mineral service. Today it seems strange that streamlined diesels would have spent so much time working away from the public eye in obscure freight service. *Richard Jay Solomon*

In May 1963 Central Railroad of New Jersey baby-face DR 4-4-1500s growl across a highway overpass with freight in tow. CNJ's Baldwin road diesels were among the longest to survive in service under their original ownership without repowering. *Richard Jay Solomon*

New York Central was one of three railroads to order Baldwin's four-motor road-freight diesel model DR 4-4-1500 in the baby-face body style. Although they looked substantially different, the early freight-service shark-nose units—those on B trucks rated at 1,500 horsepower—carried the same model designation as their baby-face counterparts. Later sharks were rated at 1,600 horsepower, designated model RF-16. On June 21, 1953, an A-B-A set of DR 4-4-1500s works Central's Selkirk hump yard. *Jim Shaughnessy*

Above: New York Central bought two A-B-A sets of Baldwin's DR-6-4-1500 baby-face streamlined passenger diesels. The only other taker was Seaboard Air Line. Central's were poorly regarded. Originally they rode on Commonwealth trucks and were known as "Gravel Gerties" because of their rough ride. Later the trucks were replaced, as was Baldwin's prime mover. Seen here in Collinwood after repowering with EMD's reliable 567 engine, Baldwin No. 3606 is paired with a similarly repowered Fairbanks-Morse "Erie-built." *J. William Vigrass*

Opposite top: Pennsy's big sharks—the 2,000-horsepower units carried on A1A trucks, designated as class BP20s by the railroad and model DR-6-4-2000 by the builder—were built in 1948 for long-distance passenger service but were bumped within a decade to lesser duties. In June 1964, BP20 No. 5773 hits a grade crossing on the New York & Long Branch as the rain lashes down. Slow film mandated creative photographic technique, so Richard Jay Solomon used his Leica range finder to pan the distinctive Baldwin profile. *Richard Jay Solomon*

Opposite bottom: Between assignments in suburban service on New Jersey's New York & Long Branch route, Pennsylvania Railroad DR-6-4-2000 No. 5770 rests at a diesel shop in the New Jersey Meadows on May 10, 1959. This date was the ninetieth anniversary of the famous "golden spike," when Central Pacific and Union Pacific met at Promontory, Utah—not that this mattered one iota to Pennsy or the lowly shark! *Richard Jay Solomon*

Chapter 3

Electro-Motive

Electro-Motive

eneral Motors' Electro-Motive Division—commonly known by the initials EMD after 1940—was the largest producer of diesel-electrics in the three decades following World War II. Its products effectively defined the diesel-electric as a road locomotive, and its innovations proved to American railroads that diesels could match the performance of steam while substantially lowering operating costs.

In 1930, General Motors acquired internal combustion engine manufacturer Winton Engine Company, along with gas-electric railcar designer Electro-Motive Company. During the next few years, these new GM subsidiaries refined diesel-electric locomotive technology and established the lightweight streamlined diesel-power car. The company rapidly adapted this technology for use as a standalone locomotive. As its technology and business matured, Electro-Motive developed diesel-electric switchers, then high-speed passenger and heavy freight locomotives, and finally road switchers.

Keys to GM's success included compact, high-output, two-cycle engine designs; a carefully thought-out design process that ensured maximum component reliability and compatibility; automotive-like production processes that minimized per-unit costs and kept engineering differences between models to a minimum; successful marketing; attractive locomotives; and attentive customer service.

Electro-Motive's first diesel efforts were custom-designed power cars for lightweight, articulated streamlined passenger trains. Yet, at the time, switchers were the largest commercial diesel-electric market, and in 1936, Electro-Motive began production of standard end-cab diesel switchers.

In 1937, Electro-Motive introduced its streamlined E-units for fast road passenger service. The E-unit's truss-supported carbody was integral to the structure of the locomotive and was universally adopted as the standard for diesel road units of the early steam-to-diesel transition period. Initially powered by a pair of Winton diesels, the early E-units were rated at 1,800 horsepower per unit and typically operated with one cab-equipped "A" unit leading one or two cab-less "B" units. All E-units rode on a pair of A1A six-wheel trucks (outside axles powered and center axle unpowered) designed by Martin Blomberg, who employed a system of outside swing hangers using both elliptical and helical springs to provide great stability at speed.

In 1938, Electro-Motive introduced the more reliable 567 diesel engine in place of Winton 201A diesel, and pairs of 12-cylinder, 1,000-horsepower 567s were used in the E3 through E6 models. EMD introduced the much-improved E7 in 1945, and it soon proved the bestselling passenger locomotive of the postwar period. Always looking to improve its line, EMD succeeded its E7 with the 2,250-horsepower E8 in 1949. In turn, this model was succeeded by the 2,400-horsepower E9 in 1955. Although the most powerful of E-units, with the longest production run of any E model, the E9 had lower production totals than either the E7 or E8 due to the sharp decline in intercity passenger services.

The FT model freight diesel was Electro-Motive's most influential locomotive. Quietly introduced in 1939, it soon demonstrated Electro-Motive's exceptional diesel-electric capabilities in heavy road-freight service and set the standard for road diesels for the next a decade. Like the E-unit, the FT used a carbody design, but each unit was powered by a single 16-cylinder 567 engine and rode on four-wheel Blomberg-designed trucks.

In its original configuration, the FT was designed to operate as an A-B-B-A four-unit set rated at 5,400 horsepower. The FT remained in production through 1945, when it was succeeded by the more powerful and more reliable F3 model. Where the individual FT unit was rated at 1,350 horsepower, each F3 was rated at 1,500 horsepower. In 1949, the F3 was succeeded by the even more reliable F7, a model that proved one of Electro-Motive's most popular postwar types. This was supplanted in 1954 by the 1,750-horsepower F9. Although the F-unit was originally aimed at the freight market, EMD introduced several variations designed for passenger work: FP7/FP9s featured larger steam generators necessary for passenger-car heating, while the FL9 was a dual-mode type ordered exclusively by the New Haven Railroad for service in New York City third-rail territory.

EMD did not make a serious effort to compete for road-switcher sales until it introduced the four-motor "general purpose" GP7 in 1949. The GP7's exceptional versatility rapidly displaced orders for the more specialized models in the early 1950s. In 1954, EMD introduced the GP9, an improved road switcher rated at 1,750 horsepower that proved significantly more reliable than earlier designs. This became one of the company's most popular locomotives; some still work short lines in 2010. Electro-Motive also offered six-

Previous pages:
Electro-Motive's F-unit is one of the twentieth century's most iconic locomotives. Thousands of these locomotives hauled trains all across North America. In 2009, Wabash F7A No. 1189 and Norfolk Southern's executive Fs pose for photographers at the Monticello Railway Museum at Monticello, Illinois. *Chris Guss*

Metra F40C No. 614 approaches Chicago's A2 Tower in June 2004 where former Milwaukee Road lines cross those of the former Chicago & North Western. Externally, F40Cs had more in common with the F45 than with the F40PH design of the mid-1970s. A pair of Metra F40PH-2s can be seen on the tracks beyond. *Brian Solomon.*

On August 21, 1994, Wisconsin & Southern GP9 No. 4491, facing long hood first, rests at the west end of the former Milwaukee Road line to Prairie du Chien, Wisconsin. This old Electro-Motive locomotive began life as a Rock Island GP18 but was later heavily rebuilt as a GP9. *Brian Solomon*

Gulf, Mobile & Ohio's *Alton Limited* departs St. Louis for Chicago led by a pair of EMD E7s on July 22, 1958. The E7 was EMD's most popular passenger locomotive. *Richard Jay Solomon*

motor road switchers, initially with its "special duty" SD7, later followed by the SD9, and then more powerful models.

By the late 1950s, EMD was focusing production on more powerful road switchers. It introduced the 2,000-horsepower GP20 in 1961, followed by the 2,250-horsepower GP30 in 1962, and the 2,500-horsepower GP35/SD35 in 1963. Electro-Motive's introduction of the more powerful and more reliable 645 series engine in the mid-1960s resulted in the 3,000-horsepower GP40/SD40 and the

3,600-horsepower SD45. The high-horsepower units achieved greater power through application of a turbocharger; however, EMD also offered the 2,000-horsepower GP38/SD38 with a normally aspirated engine. These 645-engine diesels set new standards for reliability. In the 1970s, the six-motor SD40/SD40-2 emerged as the preferred North American locomotive. Thousands of this model were ordered, and it brought an end to many of the older and more specialized locomotives featured in these pages.

Above: Electro-Motive diesels were by far the most common of the postwar period. Working in Chicago on March 22, 1973, is Norfolk & Western NW2 switcher No. 2018—originally Wabash No. 2806. In the distance is Chesapeake & Ohio GP7 road switcher No. 5774. *R. R. Richardson photo, Doug Eisele collection*

Opposite top: Western Pacific NW2 No. 608 rests at the Western Pacific Railroad Museum at Portola, California, on May 10, 2008. This model was Electro-Motive's standard 1,000-horsepower switcher and offered for 10 years beginning in 1939. Today, No. 608 is one of many preserved vintage diesels displayed at Portola. *Brian Solomon*

Opposite bottom: An Erie-Lackawanna NW2 rests outside of the former Erie Railroad shops at Hornell, New York, on February 13, 1973. Many railroads began dieselization with the acquisition of switchers in the 1930s and later sought road diesels during World War II. Erie was among the lines that bought Electro-Motive's FT for freight service during the war. *Doug Eisele*

In April 1991, two boys watch Southern Pacific SW1500 No. 2623 work industrial trackage on the Northwestern Pacific at Petaluma, California. SP was among the last railroads to order a large fleet of new switchers, and the railroad continued to encourage lineside carload traffic by building industrial parks along its lines into the 1970s. *Brian Solomon*

Southern Pacific's switchers were a common sight around its western system. In October 1990, SP SW1500 No. 2635 works the Cal-Train terminal at Seventh and King streets in San Francisco. SP remained the contract operator of San Francisco Peninsula "commute" trains until 1992 and thus continued to provide a San Francisco–based switcher at the passenger terminal. *Brian Solomon*

Southern Pacific was famous for its "full-house" lighting on diesel-electric locomotives. SP SW1500 No. 2530 features laterally mounted headlights (right), red oscillating lights on either side of the cab door, and a red warning oscillating light above the door. The red oscillating light would only be actuated in the event of a sudden loss of air-pipe pressure caused by an emergency airbrake application and was intended to warn other train crews that the train was in trouble and potentially derailed. *Brian Solomon*

The westbound *California Zephyr* makes its scheduled station stop at Denver Union Station in 1966 to pick up passengers and exchange the Burlington E-units that brought the train from Chicago with Rio Grande F7s for the trip over the Rockies. To the right of the *Zephyr* are a Rio Grande EMD SW1200 and a World War II–vintage Burlington Alco S-2 switcher. *Richard Jay Solomon*

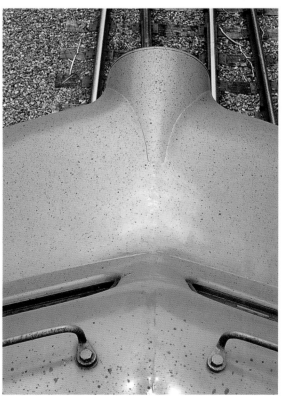

Above: Wabash was a Midwestern railroad linking the gateway cities of Buffalo, Chicago, and Kansas City. Its main line between Buffalo/Niagara Falls and Detroit, Michigan, crossed Ontario, so Wabash had a fleet of Canadian-built F7As. Wabash's F7A No. 1189 has been preserved and restored by the Monticello Railway Museum at Monticello, Illinois. *Brian Solomon*

Left: Electro-Motive's distinctive styling gave its locomotives a modern streamlined appearance. This unusual angle looks down on the nose of privately owned former Alaska Railroad F7A No. 1508, working on the Adirondack Scenic Railroad. *Brian Solomon*

Among the most unusual Electro-Motive units operated by Rock Island were the streamlined LWT12 locomotive power cars for the lightweight trains built in the mid-1950s. Seen here is Rock Island's lone TALGO train built for the Rock's *Jet Rocket*. Electro-Motive built only three LWT12 locomotives; the other two powered General Motors' *Aerotrain*s, which tested on the Pennsylvania Railroad, New York Central, and Union Pacific before being sold to the Rock. *Richard Jay Solomon*

The beautiful and the ugly posed nose to nose: Rock Island F-unit No. 310 and BL2 No. 425 face each other at Blue Island on July 18, 1958. In the late 1940s, Electro-Motive followed the lead established by Alco and introduced this 1,500-horsepower road-switcher model. The odd-looking BL1/BL2 was essentially an F3A in a modified carbody better suited for switching. *Richard Jay Solomon*

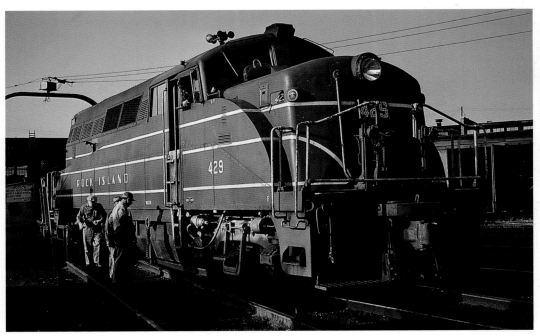

Few were the number of Electro-Motive BL2s—only 52 were built between 1947 and 1948—yet this unusual model found a great variety of work, from hauling potatoes in northern Maine to working branch lines in the Midwest and serving Rock Island in commuter service. At the end of a Chicago suburban run, Rock Island BL2 No. 429 rests at the Blue Island on July 18, 1958. *Richard Jay Solomon*

New Haven Railroad FL9s Nos. 2008 and 2012 race through South Norwalk working toward New Haven, Connecticut, on July 1963. New Haven's dual-mode FL9s were largely assigned to Boston–New York trains to eliminate the need for engine changes where steam or diesel power was exchanged for electric. *Richard Jay Solomon*

New Haven FL9s at Cos Cob on June 27, 1959. Electro-Motive's FL9 was a unique design, with specifications carefully tailored for New Haven's unusual service requirements. Among its unusual features was its dual-mode propulsion that allowed it to work as a diesel-electric or to draw power from the lineside third rail. *Richard Jay Solomon*

Repainted New Haven Railroad FL9 is seen with Waterbury, Connecticut, station's famous clock tower. In the 1980s, the Connecticut Department of Transportation paid to have four FL9s rebuilt and restored into their original New Haven livery for work on Connecticut branch trains. *Brian Solomon*

After Penn Central assumed operation of the New Haven Railroad in 1969, the FL9 fleet was largely reassigned to work suburban services on former New York Central lines out of Grand Central Terminal. These continued in such services for the next three decades. Metro-North FL9 No. 2041 leads a push-pull consist northward on the Hudson Line at the Breakneck Ridge tunnels on June 15, 1997. *Brian Solomon*

One of the more unusual late-era applications for former New Haven FL9s has been for seasonal passenger services on the old Maine Central Rockland Branch between Rockland, Bath, and New Brunswick, Maine. Maine Eastern FL9 No. 489 goes for a spin on the turntable at Rockland, Maine, after completing its day's work. *Brian Solomon*

In August 2007, Maine Eastern's FL9 No. 489 leads the railroad's passenger train at the Rockland, Maine, terminal. This was one of several FL9s operated by Amtrak on its Empire Corridor trains through the mid-1990s. Amtrak required third rail–equipped diesels to operate into the New York City terminals via the Hudson River route, although in later years the locomotives rarely worked in their electric mode. *Brian Solomon*

In its heyday, St. Louis Union Station was a crossroads of commerce. On July 22, 1958, train No. 15, the *Zephyr-Rocket*, departs St. Louis behind a Burlington E7A. Electro-Motive's E7 was the bestselling passenger locomotive of the postwar era and was bought by many railroads to supplant aging Pacific-type steam locomotives on named passenger trains. *Richard Jay Solomon*

July 27, 1958, finds a classic lineup of vintage diesels at Cincinnati Union Terminal's engine house. This photo clearly demonstrates styling differences between Electro-Motive's early production E-unit design, which used a steeply angled slant nose, and the more familiar postwar "bulldog nose." From left to right: Louisville & Nashville E7A No. 791 (built in 1949); L&N E6A No. 771 (1942); Pennsylvania Railroad E7A No. 5873 (1949); and Cincinnati Union Terminal Lima-Hamilton 750-horsepower switcher No. 20. *Richard Jay Solomon*

A pair of Rock Island E7As lead one of the railroad's famous *Rocket* streamliners near Chicago in 1961. Rock Island didn't join Amtrak in 1971 and continued to operate a ragtag fleet of E-units in both suburban and long-distance passenger service until the mid-1970s. *Richard Jay Solomon*

A pair of Erie Lackawanna E8s labor toward Gulf Summit, New York, with an eastward freight in July 1973. After E-L discontinued long-distance passenger services, it reassigned its E-units to freight work. While these were well liked for flatland running in the Midwest, their high-speed gearing and A1A trucks were ill-suited to steep grades in the East. *Kenneth J. Buck*

Restored New York Central E8A No. 4080 is displayed at the Medina Railroad Museum at Medina, New York. It is one of two units at the museum painted in the classic New York Central lightening stripe scheme. Electro-Motive E-units represented the majority of the Central's long-distance passenger locomotives in the diesel era. *Brian Solomon*

In summer 1963, New York Central E8A No. 4052 and an E7B lead a passenger train northward (railroad direction west) along the Hudson River toward Albany below the famous Bear Mountain bridge. *Richard Jay Solomon*

Pennsylvania Railroad No. 5711 became Conrail No. 4021, one of three E8s used by Conrail for its business train. It was restored by Juniata Terminal into its 1950s scheme with its old Pennsy number. Here Pennsy E8As approach Keating, Pennsylvania, along the banks of the Susquehanna River on October 11, 2003. *Brian Solomon*

Pennsy E8A No. 5711 is near Renovo, Pennsylvania, on October 11, 2003. The Juniata-restored E8As make occasional appearances on former Pennsylvania Railroad lines. *Brian Solomon*

Introduced in 1949, Electro-Motive's E8 represented a substantial improvement over the E7. By using three-phase AC motor-operated appliances, the new model eliminated belt-driven exhaust fans and other appliances. With the addition of high-capacity steam generators, the E8 featured more effective train heating while engine output was boosted to 2,250 horsepower compared with the E7's 2,000 horsepower. *Brian Solomon*

Above: Chicago & North Western GP7s Nos. 4117 and 4141 lead the northward Jefferson Junction local toward Clyman Junction at Johnson Creek, Wisconsin, on April 19, 1995. Electro-Motive dabbled with road-switcher designs in the mid-1940s by building a handful of NW3s and NW5s and then brought out the short-lived BL2 in 1948. It was the GP7 of 1949 that properly introduced the "general purpose" road switcher to Electro-Motive's catalog. *Brian Solomon*

Opposite top: The GP7 was built in large numbers between 1949 and 1954, when the model was replaced by the more powerful, more reliable, and even more versatile GP9. At sunset on May 11, 1995, C&NW GP7s approach Clyman Junction, Wisconsin. By this time, these locomotives had more than 40 years service since leaving Electro-Motive's plant. *Brian Solomon*

Opposite bottom: Detail of C&NW GP7 No. 4174, one of several units built new for the Rock Island and acquired by C&NW in the early 1980s after Rock's demise. C&NW continued to use its classic herald up until its merger with Union Pacific in spring 1995. *Brian Solomon*

Above: Springfield Terminal No. 21 works the yard at Lawrence, Massachusetts, in June 1987. It was built in Canada for the Algoma Central in 1963 and later acquired by Maine Central, becoming its No. 450. Significantly, this was the very last GP9 built and was finished many years after Electro-Motive had supplanted the GP9 with more powerful four-motor models. *Brian Solomon*

Opposite top: Boston & Maine was among the first railroads to replace its early Electro-Motive diesels with the more reliable types offered in the mid-1950s. In 1957, it traded back its World War II–era FT fleet on new GP9s numbered 1700–1749. These units used some components recycled from the old FTs. Boston & Maine GP9 No. 1736 works a local freight in Somerville, Massachusetts, against the Boston skyline in August 1989. *Brian Solomon*

Opposite bottom: Guilford Rail System GP9 No. 45, lettered for Springfield Terminal, works a Connecticut River Line local freight at Keats Road south of Greenfield, Massachusetts, on October 18, 2004. Originally it was Boston & Maine No. 1703 (later 1803) built in 1957. The reliability and durability of Electro-Motive's general purpose diesels have given them unusually long lifespans, with some units working well into their fifth decade. *Brian Solomon*

Southern Pacific's early GP9s were painted in its very classy "Black Widow" freight livery. Notice the panel below the numberboards for easy access. SP used numberboards to display train numbers rather than locomotive numbers, as was typical on most other railroads. The train number denotes a specific service, while a locomotive number identifies the specific engine. *Bob Morris*

Southern Pacific GP9E No. 3842 and a pair of SD9Es lead a westward freight along the shore of California's San Pablo Bay at Pinole on April 18, 1993. In the 1970s, SP rebuilt many of its 567-powered GP and SD units, which allowed them to continue in revenue freight service into the 1990s. *Brian Solomon*

Southern Pacific No. 3821 is among GP9Es laying over at Watsonville Junction on SP's Coast Line. In addition to oscillating lights and fixed headlights, SP diesels typically featured classification lamps, although by the 1990s these had been blanked out. Class lamps had been necessary for the method of train movement authorization under the old timetable and train order rules. *Brian Solomon*

Central Vermont was among the last railroads in New England to entirely displace steam with diesels. Some GP9s that had worked alongside 2-8-0s survived into the early 1990s. GP9s work at Dublin Street in Palmer, Massachusetts, in December 1988. Leading local freight No. 562 is CV No. 4549 and Grand Trunk No. 4139. *Brian Solomon*

Left: CV's pair of recently rebuilt GP9s (with low short hoods) works in fresh paint near the Hospital Road crossing in Monson, Massachusetts, on December 31, 1986. *Brian Solomon*

Opposite: CV was among several railroads that traditionally designated the long hood as front. While this offered increased safety for the crew, it reduced visibility. In the mid-1980s, Central Vermont rebuilt and lowered the short hood on two of its 1950s-built GP9s, resulting in the short end becoming the front. CV No. 4559 is seen at the Dublin Street engine facility in Palmer, Massachusetts. *Brian Solomon*

Left: Central Vermont GP9 No. 4925 rests in the yard at Palmer alongside a Grand Trunk GP38. In the late 1980s and early 1990s, GP38s gradually replaced CV's aging fleet of GP9s. *Brian Solomon*

Below: Central Vermont's regular road freight operated six days a week between St. Albans, Vermont, and Palmer, Massachusetts. On July 2, 1988, five GP9s lead freight No. 444 across the Connecticut River bridge at East Northfield, Massachusetts. A speed restriction on the bridge insured the train crawled across the early twentieth-century span at 10 miles per hour. *Brian Solomon*

Southern Pacific GP20E No. 4112 leads the Woodland turn at Davis, California, in October 1989. The GP20 was Electro-Motive's early effort at producing a high-output four-motor road switcher, but it was known for turbocharger difficulties. Southern Pacific extended the life of its GP20 fleet by replacing the turbocharger with a more reliable method of engine aspiration. *Brian Solomon*

Under the gloom of a December sky, Toledo, Peoria & Western GP20s lead grain cars near Peoria, Illinois. No. 2015 wears a paint scheme inspired by the New York Central lightning stripe and adapted for TP&W by artist Mike Danneman. *Brian Solomon*

Wisconsin & Southern acquired a variety of EMD road switchers from Southern Pacific, including this old GP20E, originally SP No. 7224. Known by reporting marks WSOR, the railroad operated a network of lines in southern Wisconsin. On March 22, 1996, WSOR No. 4118 leads a freight over Wisconsin Central trackage in Waukesha. *Brian Solomon*

Although unremarkable when new, Electro-Motive's three GP18s built for New York, Susquehanna & Western in 1962 became one of the longest surviving original fleets. As late as autumn 2009, No. 1802 was still in service for the company. In October 1963, No. 1804 was working a freight in New Jersey. *Richard Jay Solomon*

Left: The application of a General Electric speedometer on this Electro-Motive-built NYS&W GP18 No. 1802 is confusing for casual observers. *Brian Solomon*

Opposite: NYS&W's GP18s were built with low short hoods. Other railroads, such as Rock Island and Norfolk & Western, bought GP18s with high short hoods. *Brian Solomon*

On July 3, 1989, a venerable Norfolk & Western high-hood GP30 leads a westward Norfolk Southern freight at Buffalo, New York. In the distance is the famous Buffalo Terminal. N&W and Southern were the only two railroads to order GP30s with the high short-hood option. *Brian Solomon*

In August 1998, former Rio Grande GP30 No. 3002 works a Union Pacific local freight at Antonito, Colorado. Rio Grande's GP30s were bought for fast freight service but ended up in slow-speed local service late in their careers. *Brian Solomon*

On March 12, 1980, Conrail GP30 No. 2247—still wearing Penn Central black—leads a freight at Overview, Pennsylvania, heading into the former Pennsylvania Railroad Enola Yard. The GP30 was powered by a 16-cylinder turbocharged 567 diesel. Turbocharging helped extract 2,250 horsepower from the 16-567, originally designed for 1,350-horsepower. *Doug Eisele*

In November 1988, a GP30 in fresh CSX paint leads a Chessie System GP40 westward over the Niagara Gorge at Niagara Falls, New York, with a Buffalo–Detroit freight. CSX's service on this route was inherited from the old Pere Marquette, a company acquired by CSX predecessor Chesapeake & Ohio in the 1940s. *Brian Solomon*

On October 4, 1984, Chesapeake & Ohio GP30 No. 3007, painted in the 1970s-inspired Chessie System livery, leads a GP9 off the former Buffalo, Rochester & Pittsburgh Belt Line on the way back to Brooks Avenue Yard in Rochester, New York. *Doug Eisele*

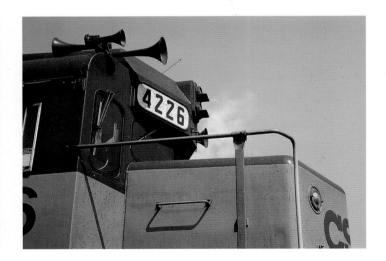

CSX predecessors Baltimore & Ohio and Chesapeake & Ohio both acquired large numbers of GP30s. CSX GP30 No. 4226 had been C&O No. 3035. It was among the first diesels painted in the CSX blue and gray livery. During the 1980s, many CSX GP30s were rebuilt and redesignated GP30Ms. Although CSX retired its last GP30 in 1997, some of the locomotives have been converted into road slugs (traction motors with ballast but no engine). *Brian Solomon*

In February 1995, New England Central assumed operations formerly handled by Canadian National Railway's Central Vermont subsidiary. GP38s 3850 and 3854 lead southward freight 608 past old mill buildings in Stafford Springs, Connecticut, in April 1998. *Brian Solomon*

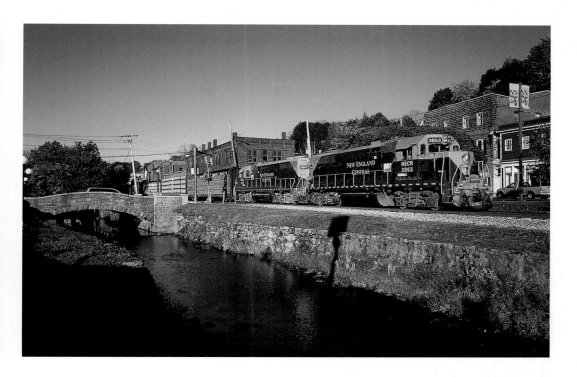

On October 13, 2006, New England Central GP38s Nos. 3853 and 3847 lead southward freight No. 608 through downtown Stafford Springs, Connecticut. New England Central serves local freight customers in southern New England and provides a through-service connection to Providence & Worcester in Connecticut. *Brian Solomon*

Approaching Belchertown, Massachusetts, in October 1998, New England Central engineer Steve Carlson works the throttle on a GP38. The 2,000-horsepower locomotive was well suited to the railroad's freight operations. *Brian Solomon*

Above: In 1972, Electro-Motive introduced its much-improved Dash 2 line that improved the electrical system used on its 645-series diesels. Most new models had the same output but offered a more reliable locomotive. The GP38-2 has remained as one of the most desirable locomotives for light freight service in North America. Wisconsin & Southern GP38-2 No. 3805 was photographed at Janesville, Wisconsin, in July 2005. *Brian Solomon*

Opposite top: Delaware & Hudson GP38s Nos. 7312 and 7304 work a local freight along the old Erie Railroad main line at Owego, New York, in October 2002. CP Rail acquired the old D&H in 1990, and these locomotives were retroactively painted into the D&H "heritage livery," originally introduced on the four Alco PA cab units D&H acquired from Santa Fe in the 1960s. *Brian Solomon*

Opposite bottom: Pittsburgh & Lake Erie GP38-2s leading a loaded Bow coal train at William Street in Buffalo. The train has just come in on Norfolk Southern's former Nickel Plate Road route and waits for a D&H crew to take it east on the old Erie Railroad. *Brian Solomon*

In June 1994, Southern Pacific SD9E No. 4411 leads a work train over Pengra Pass in the Oregon Cascades. SP bought 149 SD9s—the majority of Electro-Motive's production. Many served the railroad for the better part of four decades; most were rebuilt in-kind as SD9Es in the 1970s to extend their service lives. *Brian Solomon*

Above: In May 1990, a pair of SP SD9 "Cadillacs" catches the evening light at Grants Pass, Oregon. These smooth-riding units were regulars on the Medford–Grants Pass turn in the early 1990s before SP discontinued operations on the Siskiyou Line and sold the route to RailTex. *Brian Solomon*

Opposite: This closeup of SP SD9E No. 4372 finds it equipped with the classic SP full-lighting arrangement that includes oscillating headlights, sealed-beam headlights, and classification lamps. *Brian Solomon*

Above: Duluth, Missabe & Iron Range SD9 No. 166 was still wearing factory paint when it rested at the Wisconsin Central shops in North Fond du Lac, Wisconsin, on September 2, 1995. Ore-hauling DM&IR was a natural customer for high-tractive-effort six-motor diesels, which replaced its massive 2-8-8-4 Yellowstones in the 1950s. *Brian Solomon*

Opposite top: Chicago & North Western SD9 No. 1703 rests in Chicago near a steam-era coaling tower on July 17, 1958. "Route of the Streamliners" dates from the time when C&NW forwarded Union Pacific's famous trains from Omaha to Chicago. *Richard Jay Solomon*

Opposite bottom: On September 23, 1994, Burlington Northern SD9 No. 6150 leads a local freight at Gunn, Minnesota. In essence, Electro-Motive's SD9 was a six-motor variation of the popular GP9. Both models shared many of the same mechanical and electrical components with the obvious exception of the trucks. *Brian Solomon*

Wisconsin Central F45 No. 6651 and FP45 No. 6652 work freight No. 119 from North Fond du Lac to Green Bay, Wisconsin, at Kaukauna on April 6, 1996. Wisconsin Central acquired a handful of F45s and a sole FP45 from Santa Fe in the mid-1990s. *Brian Solomon*

Train 348 roars through Waukesha, Wisconsin, on March 22, 1996, with Wisconsin Central F45 No. 6655 in the lead on a bright, sunny day. What better reason to escape the office than to watch a freshly painted F45 roll through town? *Brian Solomon*

On May 4, 1996, Wisconsin Central F45 No. 6656 was displayed for public viewing on the East Troy Electric at Mukwonago, Wisconsin. Wisconsin Central—along with Montana Rail Link; New York, Susquehanna & Western; and Wisconsin & Southern—operated F45s acquired secondhand after Electro-Motive's 20-cylinder 645E3 prime mover had largely fallen out of favor on the larger railroads. *Brian Solomon*

New Santa Fe FP45s Nos. 105 and 104 lead the *El Capitan* in 1968. Powered by the 3,600-horsepower 20-cylinder 645E3 engine, these were among the most powerful single-unit passenger diesels of the 1960s. *Richard Jay Solomon*

Wisconsin Central FP45 No. 6652 still wears Santa Fe warbonnet paint. On September 2, 1995, it was photographed alongside WC's Algoma Central FP9 No. 1752 at North Fond du Lac shops. *Brian Solomon*

Opposite: The popular Santa Fe FP45 No. 92 is now displayed at the Illinois Railway Museum in Union, Illinois. Built in 1967 as Santa Fe No. 102, this locomotive enjoyed a 30-year career hauling passenger and freight trains before being preserved at IRM in 1997. *Brian Solomon*

Left: In the mid-1960s, Electro-Motive met Santa Fe's request for a shrouded diesel by adapting the SD45 with external cowling that shrouded the machinery. Unlike the old E- and F-units, whose carbodies were integral to their structure, the shrouds of cowl-type locomotives are non-integral. This is a windshield detail of Santa Fe F45 No. 5959. *Brian Solomon*

Below: The success of the FP45 led Santa Fe and the Great Northern to order 20-cylinder F45s solely for freight service. These looked very similar and shared most components with the FP45 designed for passenger and freight service. *Brian Solomon*

Santa Fe continued to operate its F45/FP45 fleet into the 1990s. When Santa Fe began to pare down its roster of 20-cylinder diesels, including its SD45s, it sold some F45s and one FP45 to Wisconsin Central. *Brian Solomon*

At 2:20 p.m. on January 22, 1991, Santa Fe SD45 No. 5400 storms westward at Bagdad, California, on Santa Fe's Needles District in the Mojave Desert. Electro-Motive's 20-cylinder diesels, including the SD45, F45, and SD45-2, had a distinctive, low throbbing sound that could be heard for many miles. *Brian Solomon*

Above: On June 22, 1982, Rio Grande SD45 No. 5336 and a pair of Union Pacific SD45s lead a westward Rio Grande coal train. While Rio Grande's SD45 fleet was among the longest to survive, UP's was one of the shortest. *George W. Kowanski*

Opposite: New York, Susquehanna & Western SD45 No. 3620 reveals its Burlington Northern heritage with a bit of cascade green paint visible atop the short hood. Susquehanna acquired a small fleet of former BN SD45s and F45s in the late 1980s for use on its transcontinental Sea-Land double-stack container trains. *Brian Solomon*

On December 3, 1994, Wisconsin Central SD45s ascend Byron Hill at Lost Arrow Road a few miles south of Fond du Lac, Wisconsin. For several years after Wisconsin Central was acquired by Canadian National in 2001, the railroad continued to operate SD45s in road-freight service; Byron Hill was among the last places to hear multiple SD45s hard at work, their 20-645E3 engines resonating across cornfields. *Brian Solomon*

The SD45 was visually distinguishable from other EMD six-motor road switchers by its diagonally oriented or "flared" radiator intake arrangement. WC No. 6593 is shown here at Byron, Wisconsin, on the morning of April 6, 1996. *Brian Solomon*

Wisconsin Central SD45s cross-plowed cornfields south of Byron, Wisconsin, on their way from the yards at North Fond du Lac to Chicago. WC's secondhand SD45 fleet was one of the last big fleets of 20-cylinder diesels in the United States. *Brian Solomon*

Chapter 4
Fairbanks-Morse

Fairbanks-Morse

airbanks-Morse's railroad connections date to the late nineteenth century. Early F-M railroad products consisted of track-maintenance equipment, including work cars, velocipedes, and handcars with the familiar walking-beam power lever. By 1893, F-M was selling gasoline engines for railcars, and in the early twentieth century it was building gasoline-powered railcars and small industrial gasoline-mechanical locomotives.

During the 1930s, F-M was one of several companies that benefited from research and development of compact high-output diesels for naval applications. This program resulted in F-M's unusual two-cycle opposed-piston engine. Each cylinder served a pair of pistons facing one another, obviating the need for cylinder heads, requiring fewer moving parts, and benefiting from superior heat dissipation while operating with lower piston speeds.

By 1940, F-M was the second-largest diesel engine-builder in the United States, and during World War II it provided large numbers of engines for submarines and other military applications. To accommodate its booming production, F-M greatly expanded its capacity, particularly at its Beloit,

Wisconsin, factory. In mid-1944, it entered the heavy domestic locomotive business. The War Production Board initially limited F-M to switchers, but after the war the company introduced a complete line of locomotives with configurations comparable to other builders. In several instances, F-M's offerings were significantly more powerful than competitors'. All of these locomotives were powered by variations of F-M's successful 38D8-1/8 opposed-piston design, which it manufactured in 6-, 8-, 10- and 12-cylinder varieties.

Most F-M locomotives for the domestic market were built at its Beloit plant. An exception were its first carbody types, large road diesels built between 1945 and 1949, which used bodies erected under contract by General Electric at Erie, Pennsylvania. To serve the Canadian market, F-M licensed its locomotive designs to the Canadian Locomotive Company of Kingston, Ontario.

As with the other large builders, F-M started with a moderately powered switcher, the H-10-44 (H for hood, 10 for 1,000 horsepower, and 44 for four axles and four motors), and then introduced a host of road types. Initially it offered road switchers in two four-motor varieties: the 1,500-horsepower H-15-44 and 2,000-horsepower H-20-44. The latter model was peculiar, as it featured an end-cab design more typical of slow-geared switchers but was equipped with road trucks geared for 65 miles per hour (this was the most powerful road switcher at the time). This type remained relatively obscure and was only ordered by five railroads with less than 100 units built.

F-M's initial streamlined road diesels were the aforementioned Erie-built models. These were rated at 2,000 horsepower and powered by the same 10-cylinder opposed-piston engine used in the H-20-44. In 1950, F-M introduced its much improved Consolidation line (known popularly as C-Liners). These streamlined carbody diesels were available in 11 different configurations, ranging from 1,600 to 2,400 horsepower per unit. Although similar to the Erie-built units in general appearance, they embraced a more refined exterior design. At the same time, F-M also increased its standard four-motor road switcher from 1,500 to 1,600 horsepower, a move equivalent with Alco and Baldwin improvements implemented about the same time. In 1951, F-M introduced the H-16-66 six-motor road switcher. This was supplemented in 1953 by the famed Train-Master H-24-66, a large and very powerful six-motor type rated at 2,400 horsepower per unit. Although only 127 units were sold, it was F-M's most influential model and set a high-horsepower precedent emulated more successfully by Alco, Electro-Motive, and General Electric.

F-M sold 1,256 diesel-electric locomotives, yet was the least successful of the four large diesel locomotive builders in the postwar period. It consistently held fourth place in market share until 1953, when it finally passed Baldwin. While F-M built locomotives until 1963, the vast majority of its domestic production was conducted in its first decade as a builder and it sold very few locomotives after 1957.

F-M diesels tended not to fair well on railroads that mixed F-Ms into road pools with minimal concern for their more specialized service requirements. By the mid-1960s, unmodified F-M diesels were already rare. Most were retired by the mid-1970s.

Previous pages:
Long Island Rail Road C-Liner No. 2006 basks in the evening sun on November 6, 1960, at Montauk Point, New York. The Fairbanks-Morse CPA-20-5 used an unusual B-A1A wheel arrangement to provide added support for a steam boiler at the rear of the locomotive while keeping axle weight within acceptable limits. *Richard Jay Solomon*

Pittsburgh & Lake Erie affiliate Pittsburgh, Chartiers & Youghiogheny Railway operated this orphan 1,000-horsepower F-M switcher that it purchased in 1949. PC&Y No. 1 was stored among Alcos at P&LE's shops at McKees Rocks, Pennsylvania, on July 9, 1958. *Richard Jay Solomon*

Above: Dressed to represent Southern Pacific No. 1487, complete with large oscillating headlight, this F-M H-12-44 switcher is former U.S. Army No. 1874. In October 2003, it was photographed at the Golden Gate Railway Museum at Hunters Point in San Francisco. Today, it resides with the GGRM collection at Brightside in California's Niles Canyon. *Brian Solomon*

Opposite: This interior view of the cab of former Milwaukee Road F-M H-10-44 No. 767 shows the arrangement of the control stand. Built at Beloit, Wisconsin, No. 767 is preserved in working condition at the National Railroad Museum in Green Bay, Wisconsin. Only a handful of F-M diesels have been preserved. *Brian Solomon*

Central Railroad of New Jersey, which operated one of the most eclectic diesel fleets in the United States, had several F-M models. In June 1961, CNJ H-15-44 No. 1508 leads a Jersey City–bound commuter train across the massive Newark Bay bridge at Bayonne, New Jersey. *Richard Jay Solomon*

Central Railroad of New Jersey F-M H-15-44 No. 1514 switches a suburban train at Communipaw Yards in Jersey City on April 24, 1958. At the time, some photographers may have considered the row of automobiles in the foreground an annoyance, but today they are as interesting as the curious opposed-piston diesel-electric. *Richard Jay Solomon*

Fairbanks-Morse locomotives abound in this classic photo at Jersey City on the afternoon of August 25, 1959. On the left, Central Railroad of New Jersey H-15-44 No. 1512 switches a Reading Company train, while an H-24-66 Train-Master roars out of CNJ's terminal station with a commuter train. Another F-M can be seen lurking under the train shed. *Richard Jay Solomon*

Above: Pittsburgh & West Virginia was one of only a few railroads that preferred F-M diesels over other manufacturers and in the 1950s made its transition from steam power to two-cycle opposed-piston diesels. P&WV H-20-44s Nos. 55 and 63 are shown at Rook, Pennsylvania, in 1958. Norfolk & Western absorbed the operations of P&WV in 1964. *Richard Jay Solomon*

Opposite top: By the mid-1950s, the versatility of the diesel-electric road switcher had made it the predominant type of new locomotive. P&WV H16-44 No. 91 pauses on the turntable at Rook, near Pittsburgh, Pennsylvania. This locomotive was not yet two years old when seen on July 6, 1958. Bidirectional road switchers rendered turning facilities unnecessary and simplified operations. *Richard Jay Solomon*

Opposite bottom: A pair of P&WV H-20-44s leads train 92 at Rook on July 6, 1958. P&WV's 12 H-20-44s were numbered 50–71. F-M built just 96 H-20-44s between 1947 and 1954, and P&WV was among only five railroads to purchase this unusually powerful four-motor model. Although they feature the end-cab design typically associated with low-speed switchers, the H-20-44 was geared for road service. *Richard Jay Solomon*

Above: Akron, Canton & Youngstown was an unusual industrial short line because the majority of its diesel fleet consisted of F-M road switchers, including H-16-44s (pictured), a few H-20-44s, but also a few Alco S-2s and a sole Alco RS-1. *J. William Vigrass*

Opposite top: A New Haven Railroad F-M H-16-44 road switcher and a GP9 lead a work train at Eastchester Bay, New York, on June 27, 1959. New Haven's early approach to dieselization was unusual: It bought diesels from every builder except Electro-Motive. New Haven operated several F-M models, including these road switchers. It wasn't until the mid-1950s that NH bought Electro-Motive diesels, including the custom-designed FL9s. *Richard Jay Solomon*

Opposite bottom: On July 24, 1958, Southern Railway H-16-44 No. 2148 leads a short local freight through Centralia, Illinois. F-M diesels were unusual on the Southern. It owned just 10 H-16-44s, although its Cincinnati, New Orleans & Texas Pacific subsidiary also owned some, along with a rarely photographed fleet of H-24-66 Train-Masters. *Richard Jay Solomon*

FAIRBANKS-MORSE

Central Railroad of New Jersey F-M Train-Master No. 2404 leads a Canadian Pacific 4-6-2 on an excursion in eastern Pennsylvania in October 1966. While most fans at the time were probably enthralled by the steam locomotive, it is the H-24-66 that is of greater interest today. The steam engine is still with us, while the F-M was cut up for scrap decades ago. *Richard Jay Solomon*

In July 1964, Central Railroad of New Jersey H-24-66 No. 2410 leads a three-car suburban train on the New York & Long Branch. Both Pennsylvania Railroad and CNJ provided suburban services on the NY&LB, and in the mid-1960s this route was a bastion of unusual and eclectic diesel power. Today, NJ Transit provides passenger services on the line. *Richard Jay Solomon*

Central Railroad of New Jersey, along with Southern Pacific, assigned 2,400-horsepower F-M Train-Masters to suburban passenger services where frequent stops meant that locomotives needed to get up to speed quickly to maintain schedules. *Richard Jay Solomon*

An A-B-B-A set of New York Central's Fairbanks-Morse CFA-20-4 C-Liners roar eastbound through the deep cut east of Washington Station, Massachusetts, on the old Boston & Albany route on August 22, 1954. Leading is No. 5004. The Central bought several C-Liner models in the early 1950s, but the locomotives remained relatively obscure among the hoards of Electro-Motives and Alcos. *Robert A. Buck*

New York Central C-Liners Nos. 5007 and 5009 work east at Tower SM at the east end of the enormous Alfred H. Smith Memorial Bridge across the Hudson Valley at Castleton, New York, on August 22, 1954. For a few years from the late-1940s through the mid-1950s, F-M diesels were commonly assigned to the Boston & Albany route. *Robert A. Buck*

This nose view shows New York Central C-Liner No. 6603 as it looked in the late-era "cigar band" livery. Built in 1952, this was one of seven CFA-16-4 models built for Central. Where Central's 5000-series CFA-20-4s were rated at 2,000 horsepower per unit, these similar-looking C-Liners were rated at just 1,600 horsepower. In 1960, Electro-Motive rebuilt these C-Liners by replacing the F-M diesels with their own engines. *Jim Shaughnessy*

Milwaukee Road ordered 15 powerful Fairbanks-Morse "Erie-builts" for service on its *Olympian Hiawatha*. They were assembled at GE's Erie, Pennsylvania, plant between December 1945 and March 1947, and they originally were adorned with an attractive stainless-steel styling on the nose. All the Erie-built locomotives rode on A1A trucks and were powered by Fairbanks-Morse's 2,000-horsepower 10-cylinder opposed-piston diesel. No. 12A is shown at Chicago's Western Avenue Yard on July 17, 1958. *Richard Jay Solomon*

A Canadian National C-Liner rests among a variety of other diesels and stored steam locomotives at Montreal's Turcot Yards on May 4, 1958. F-M's locomotives for the Canadian market were assembled by the Canadian Locomotive Company at Kingston, Ontario. Canadian National and Canadian Pacific both bought C-Liners and F-M road switchers. *Richard Jay Solomon*

A pair of New York Central C-Liners work eastward through Warren, Massachusetts, on a lovely autumn morning in the early 1950s. *Warren St. George photo, courtesy of Robert A. Buck*

Chapter 5

General Electric

General Electric

Beginning in the 1890s, General Electric was among the pioneers in the development of heavy electric locomotives and related technology. In the early years of the twentieth century, GE built gas-electric railcars and dabbled in gas-electric locomotives. During the World War I period, GE attempted to construct small diesel-electrics but gave up before achieving commercial success. Then, in the mid-1920s, GE entered a consortium with Alco and Ingersoll-Rand in the production of small diesel-electric switchers that are generally regarded as the world's first commercially successful diesel locomotives. It might seem strange that despite GE's important achievements in the formative years of diesel development, it opted to remain largely a supplier and contract producer of diesel electric technology during the crucial changeover period from steam to diesel. Yet, its roll as Alco's partner between 1940 and 1953 gave GE a satisfactory level of design control in the construction of diesels. These locomotives were jointly marketed as Alco-GE products but constructed by Alco at Schenectady, New York.

During this period, GE did manufacture a line of small switchers designed for industrial, yard, and branch-line applications at its own Schenectady plant. Best known of these were its 44-ton center cab, intended for one-man operation on common carrier railroads, and an end-cab 70-ton model. During this same time period, GE continued to build heavy straight electrics and gas-turbine electric road locomotives at its Erie, Pennsylvania, plant. Interestingly, GE's heavy electrics and turbines shared styling similarities with the Alco FA/PA diesels as a result of GE providing industrial design for Alco's road diesel carbodies.

It was logical for GE to develop its own line of heavy road diesels after it parted ways with Alco in 1953, and during the mid-1950s GE quietly worked at research and development of high-horsepower locomotives. It bought the Cooper-Bessemer FDL diesel design and adapted it for high-output locomotive service. Initially, GE focused its road diesel types on the export market, but in 1959 and 1960, it debuted its Universal Series for domestic applications. First was its famed U25B, a four-motor 2,500-horsepower road-switcher type aimed at fast freight service. At the time of its introduction, this was the most powerful single-unit diesel-electric on the domestic market, and it offered serious competition to models built by Alco and EMD (by that time Baldwin and Fairbanks-Morse had exited the domestic locomotive market). In 1963, GE introduced a six-motor model called the U25C. GE soon claimed the position of second-most productive diesel locomotive manufacturer, edging out its one-time partner.

During the 1960s, many railroads were replacing postwar diesels with more powerful and more reliable locomotives. Part of this strategy was buying new units that would do the same work as two of the older units, and all of the manufacturers gradually increased the output of their standard models. When in the mid-1960s Alco and EMD matched the output of their products to meet or exceed that of GE, the latter introduced new, more powerful models. In late 1965 and early 1966, GE introduced new 2,800-horsepower units to supplant its 2,500-horsepower units. Then, a year later, it introduced 3,000-horsepower models, matching the output then offered by Electro-Motive's GP40 and SD40. GE's U30C proved to be its most successful U

model with nearly 600 units sold to domestic lines. While 3,000-horsepower models remained in production through the mid-1970s, GE also offered 3,300-horsepower and 3,600-horsepower road freight types: models U33C and U36C that competed with Alco's C-636 and Electro-Motive's successful SD45, as well as U33B and U36B four-motor types.

While General Electric initially addressed the most lucrative segment of the American locomotive market—road freight locomotives—on request of customers, it adapted its Universal designs for passenger applications, notably building U28CG and U30CG models for Santa Fe with steam generators and U34CH with head-end power capabilities for Erie-Lackawanna.

Although in the 1960s and 1970s, high-horsepower locomotives drew a significant demand, some railroads still required locomotives of more nominal output. For these applications, GE offered the four-motor U23B and six-motor U23C, both rated at 2,250 horsepower. The U23B, which remained in production until 1977, sold 425 units domestically, making it the second-most common four-motor U-boat.

Above: New Hampshire–based Claremont & Concord traditionally operated remnants of a light Boston & Maine branch and portions of a one-time electric interurban line in the vicinity of Claremont, New Hampshire. *Jim Shaughnessy*

Opposite top: Middletown & New Jersey GE 44-ton switcher No. 1 leads an excursion in September 1962. This 380-horsepower switcher was built for the Middletown & Unionville. Typical of lightweight GE switchers, it was designed for one-man operation. *Richard Jay Solomon*

Opposite bottom: The lateral symmetry and balanced designed of GE's 44-ton diesels is anomalous in American practice, where diesel locomotives have tended to use off-center designs. Restored Pennsylvania Railroad GE 44-ton switcher No. 9331 is at Strasburg, Pennsylvania. *Brian Solomon*

Above: General Electric's initial entry into the domestic heavy road-switcher market was its famed U25B. At the time of its debut in 1959, the 2,500-horsepower U25B was the most powerful single-engine diesel-electric in the United States and designed for fast freight service. Chesapeake & Ohio U25B No. 2528 rests at Sloan, New York, in December 1968. *Doug Eisele*

Left: Southern Pacific U25B No. 3100 was built by General Electric in 1963 as SP No. 7508, one of 68 U25Bs ultimately operated by SP. In their heyday, SP's U25Bs were assigned primarily to road freights east of Los Angeles on the Sunset Route. No. 3100 is seen here at the Orange Empire Railway Museum near Perris, California. *Brian Solomon*

Conrail U25B No. 2612 and two other Universal Series GE "U-boats" lead a freight across the Susquehanna River on the famous Rockville bridge on October 20, 1979. Conrail operated one of the largest rosters of U-boats, inheriting a variety of models from its predecessors and buying locomotives new from GE in the mid-1970s. After GE phased out its U-boat line, Conrail remained one of its better customers and acquired large numbers Dash 7 and Dash 8 models. *Doug Eisele*

Above: Erie Lackawanna operations on the old Erie main line were conducive to high-horsepower road switchers, and in the 1960s EL turned to all three remaining builders for powerful diesels, including U25B No. 2502, shown at Port Jervis, New York, in October 1974. *George W. Kowanski*

Opposite top: Erie Lackawanna U25Bs Nos. 2507 and 2518 lead a short westward freight through the crossovers at East Hornell, New York, on October 27, 1975. This train has just sprinted up the famed Canisteo River Valley, a remote and exceptionally scenic location that had served the old Erie as conduit of commerce since the 1850s. *Bill Dechau photo, Doug Eisele collection*

Opposite bottom: Erie Lackawanna U25B No. 2513 is seen at Hornell, New York, on September 21, 1975. Hornell owed its prosperity to the Erie Railroad, which located locomotive shops, divisional offices, dispatchers, and freight yards around the town. The downgrading of the old Erie route following the creation of Conrail in 1976 hasn't been kind to communities such as Hornell, their heydays long since past. *Doug Eisele*

359

Above: Conrail U23B No. 2797 leads an eastward freight at Rotterdam Junction New York in June 1989. Sister locomotive, Conrail No. 2798, was the last domestic U-boat built and has been preserved in working order on the Naugatuck Railroad in Connecticut. *Brian Solomon*

Opposite top: In the 1960s and 1970s, Delaware & Hudson looked to both Alco and GE for new high-horsepower units. However, not all its new diesels were high-output models. It bought the more moderately powered U23B for road service as well. On September 12, 1982, a trio of GE U23Bs, led by No. 2304, works a westward freight at Big Flats, New York, on the former Erie Railroad main line. As a condition of the creation of Conrail, D&H was granted trackage rights on the old Erie between Binghamton and Buffalo, New York. *Doug Eisele*

Opposite bottom: Penn Central U23B No. 2740 kicks up the snow as it works east on the former New York Central Water Level Route near East Rochester, New York, on February 17, 1973. By the mid-1970s, the New York Central was primarily a heavy-freight corridor. *R. R. Richardson photo, Doug Eisele collection*

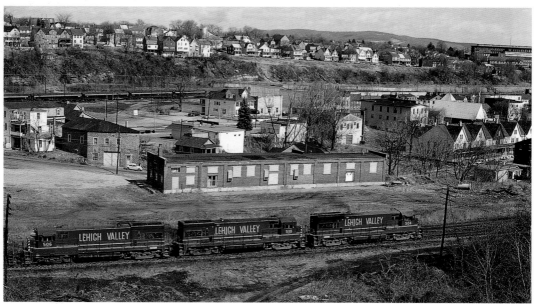

Above: Shortly after Lehigh Valley's U23Bs were delivered in radiant "Cornell red," Lehigh Valley was absorbed into Conrail. LV *Apollo-2* works east at Laurel Run, Pennsylvania. The Lehigh Valley route was one of several duplicate routes connecting the New York City metro area with the Niagara Frontier. Under Conrail, its route was truncated and much of it downgraded or abandoned. *George W. Kowanski*

Opposite top: Lehigh Valley's premier freight was its *Apollo* piggyback train. In March 1976, its eastward *Apollo-2* exits Pennsylvania's White Haven Tunnel behind new General Electric U23B No. 504. *George W. Kowanski*

Opposite bottom: Three clean Lehigh Valley U23Bs lead the *Apollo-2* eastbound at Phillipsburg, New Jersey. These moderately powered four-motor GE diesels were well suited to Lehigh Valley's graded operations. *George W. Kowanski*

Above: The merger of New York Central, the Pennsy, and the New Haven resulted in an eclectic mix of motive power, all of which was painted in Penn Central's dreary black livery. GE U30B No. 2865, Alco RS27 No. 2402, and a U25B haul an eastward freight east of Rochester, New York's Goodman Street Yard on March 12, 1974. *Bill Dechau photo, Doug Eisele collection*

Opposite top: The Penn Central bankruptcy ultimately resulted in the creation of Conrail. In August 1970, PC U33B No. 2895 and a GP38 lead a westward freight through the old Pennsylvania Railroad tunnels at Gallitzin. *George W. Kowanski*

Opposite bottom: GE's U30B matched Electro-Motive's GP40 in output but not reliability. On November 16, 1974, Penn Central U30B No. 2880, a U33B, and a U33C roar westward at Rochester, New York, with symbol freight VB-1. The Penn Central and these old GE diesels are all just a memory now. Today, CSX operates the old Water Level Route, largely with modern 4,400-horsepower GE diesels that are far more reliable than these beasts from the 1970s. *Doug Eisele*

Above: D&H U30C No. 712 leads eastward symbol freight NE2 over Richmondville Hill near Warnerville, New York, on October 13, 1976. D&H operated a fleet of six-motor GEs, including both U30Cs and U33Cs. *George W. Kowanski*

Opposite top: Boston & Maine joined Maine Central (MEC) under Guilford control in 1983. When Guilford acquired a group of secondhand SD40s and a sole U30C from Detroit Edison in the mid-1980s, it assigned the Electro-Motive units to MEC and the six-motor GE to B&M—an anomalous addition to B&M's otherwise four-motor fleet. *Brian Solomon*

Opposite bottom: On May 7, 1988, B&M U30C No. 663, former Detroit Edison No. 012, works eastward through the Canisteo Valley at Newcomb Road near Addison, New York, leading Delaware & Hudson symbol freight DHT-4. This Sealand container train utilized D&H trackage rights over Conrail's former Erie main lines between Buffalo and Binghamton in a complex arrangement that forwarded the containers to New Jersey for distribution. *Brian Solomon*

Above: Two Delaware & Hudson U33Cs bracket Maine Central U23B—formerly a D&H unit—on a westward freight approaching Dixons Crossing near Attica, New York. In 1976, D&H's trackage rights on Conrail's former Erie Railroad route between Binghamton and Buffalo boosted traffic on this orphaned route. *Brian Solomon*

Opposite top: In Conrail's early years, it operated a faded rainbow fleet of locomotives inherited from its predecessor lines. On August 20, 1977, a former Penn Central U33C leads a former Reading Company U30C west at Lincoln Park in Rochester, New York. *Doug Eisele*

Opposite bottom: On December 12, 1971, Erie Lackawanna U33C No. 3315 works west with two 20-cylinder EMDs on the old Erie Railroad main line near Waverly, New York. EL bought a variety of high-horsepower six-motor road switchers for road freight service to give it a competitive edge with its primary competitor, Penn Central. Yet, after EL was folded into Conrail in 1976, freight traffic was focused on former PC routes and much of the EL route was downgraded. *Bill Dechau, Doug Eisele*

EL acquired these big GE units specifically for suburban passenger work on nonelectrified routes radiating from Hoboken. In later years, NJ Transit inherited EL's units but continued to base them in Hoboken on former EL routes. NJ Transit U34CH No. 4167 rests between commuter runs on the former Erie at Suffern, New York, in March 1989. *Brian Solomon*

Erie Lackawanna was the only railroad to acquire GE's model U34CH. This passenger-service six-motor worked lines out of the former Lackawanna Terminal in Hoboken. In June 1971, EL No. 3359 was only a few months old when it led a westward suburban run on the old Erie Railroad main line at Waldwick, New Jersey. *George W. Kowanski*

Erie Lackawanna's 32 U34CH diesels were paid for by the New Jersey Department of Transportation and thus wore an unusual variation of the EL livery. These locomotives ultimately served NJ Transit, which assumed operations of commuter rail lines in the state in the early 1980s. The U34CH was a variation of the U36C with head-end power provisions for passenger-car heating and lighting. *George W. Kowanski*

Modern Diesel Power

601 ⊗ Ontario

Introduction

Introduction

First, some terminology. When we speak of a modern *locomotive*, we refer to the entire machine. North American diesel-electric locomotives are powered by a diesel engine that is coupled to a generator/alternator, which in turn powers electric traction motors that turn the locomotive's powered axles. Although *engine* is often used to describe the entire locomotive, in this book it refers specifically to the prime mover (i.e., the diesel engine) inside the locomotive. Since two or more diesel locomotives are routinely used to haul trains, individual locomotives are referred to as *units*.

During the 1960s, a power race between North American locomotive manufacturers resulted in the doubling of horsepower offered by typical one-engine, single-unit diesel-electric locomotives, while massive "double diesels" pushed the single unit to more than 6,000 horsepower (although only Union Pacific and Southern Pacific availed themselves of these monsters). In the 1970s, locomotive builders focused on refining designs to improve reliability rather than boosting output. During the 1980s,

demands for improved fuel economy and greater reliability were met through advances in microprocessor technology, while onboard computers and advanced wheel-slip control improved performance through tighter management of locomotive systems.

In the late 1980s and 1990s, trends toward improved crew safety resulted in the wide-scale adoption of the North American Safety Cab on locomotives built for service in the United States, thus greatly changing the outward appearance of locomotives. In the late 1980s and early 1990s, single-engine output was pushed to 4,400 horsepower using existing technologies. During this phase of development, improvements to electrical systems, combined with efforts to speed the manufacturing process (and a desire by some railroads to employ fewer locomotive types), effectively eliminated the cost advantages once offered by four-motor freight types versus six-motor types. The last new high-horsepower, four-motor road-freight diesels were built in 1994. Since then, virtually all new road-freight diesels have had six axles.

The most important innovation of the early 1990s was the practical development

An EMD-built DM30AC belonging to Long Island Rail Road hums on the platform at Jamaica, New York, in March 2003. *Brian Solomon*

of three-phase alternating current traction systems by both Electro-Motive and General Electric. The technological advances necessary to make them practical in the rigorous North American locomotive environment required intensive investment of time, skills, and resources. Both manufacturers needed substantial interest from railroads to ensure they would recoup their investment.

Three-phase AC motors are virtually free from limitations associated with DC motors when operating at maximum load (DC motors are limited by short time ratings to keep them from overheating). Additionally, three-phase AC motors offer superior wheel-slip control and extended-range dynamic braking, both of which greatly aid operation of heavy trains in graded territory while reducing costs. Because AC locomotives offer the ability to operate at maximum load at virtually any speed with minimal risk of motor damage or stalling, they were viewed as ideal for movement of heavy unit coal trains. Railroads seeking to reduce operating costs for this valuable traffic were willing to take the risk and placed significant orders for AC traction, thus allowing for its refinement.

Where EMD initially worked with Burlington Northern, GE partnered with CSX. Each manufacturer went about AC traction a different way. EMD teamed with

Previous pages:
Iowa Interstate General Electric ES44ACs wait with a freight at Blue Island, Illinois, as a Chicago Metra MP36PH-3S shoves east with a commuter train. High-horsepower freight units and specially designed passenger models are the two most common varieties of modern diesel-electric locomotives working North American railroads. *Marshall W. Beecher*

the German firm Siemens in the adaptation of European technology to American operating conditions, while General Electric refined the technology independently. The primary electrical difference between EMD's and GE's AC-traction systems is in the arrangements of the inverters—banks of high-tech electrical equipment that convert direct current to a form of modulated, three-phase alternating current for traction. The EMD-Siemens AC control system uses two inverters, one for each truck (one inverter controls three motors); General Electric uses six inverters per locomotive, which permits individual axle control and thus enables higher tractive effort while affording greater reliability.

In the mid-1990s, both manufacturers built both AC- and DC-traction locomotives in the 4,000- to 4,400-horsepower range while simultaneously advancing technology for the production of 6,000-horsepower single-engine diesels. To achieve this, both EMD and GE developed new diesel engines capable of much greater output. The theory behind a single 6,000-horsepower locomotive was based on unit reduction and component reduction. As the fleets of 1960s- and 1970s-era 3,000-horsepower diesels approached retirement age, it was expected that railroads could replace two retired locomotives with one. While both manufacturers produced commercial 6,000-horsepower locomotives, the anticipated market for these types didn't develop and relatively few were sold.

In the last decade, locomotive development has been driven largely by more stringent air-quality standards. Manufacturers have faced the challenge of reducing the volume of pollutants emitted by diesel engines while maintaining high fuel economy without sacrificing output or reliability. Because one method of reducing emissions is through improved cooling, the most modern diesel-electrics are typified by their enormous radiators at the back of the locomotive body. Other design influences affecting new locomotive types are crash-worthiness standards intended to better protect crews and prevent fuel leakage in the event of collisions, and the need to equip locomotives with modern signaling equipment necessary for positive train control.

During the last decade, passenger locomotives, once the domain of the large builders, have been built largely by smaller manufacturers. Likewise, lower horsepower diesels used for switching have been built by a variety of smaller companies.

This book focuses on successful new locomotive designs introduced since 1980, with an emphasis on types built since the advent of microprocessor controls. Although a great variety of models in operation on North American railroads are depicted, this book is not intended as a comprehensive identification guide.

Opposite: State-of-the-art in the mid-1980s, older General Electric Dash 8s are now considered "classics." On May 12, 2007, Norfolk Southern C39-8 No. 8554 leads a westward freight across the former Erie Railroad trestle at Portage, New York. *Brian Solomon*

Chapter 1
General Electric

General Electric

I n the 1980s, General Electric emerged as America's foremost diesel builder. Key to its commercial advantage were diesel-electric technologies that enabled GE to deliver substantially more reliable locomotives, known as its new Dash 8 line.

In the 1980s, computer technology had matured to the point where it could withstand the rigors of a locomotive operating environment, while being small enough for convenient placement within the confines of a modern locomotive. The Dash 8 design used three computers: one to oversee locomotive control functions, one to manage the main alternator, and one to control the fans and blower motors. The computers run programs that optimize performance for respective components while protecting key systems from overuse. Diagnostic features track and record component performance while monitoring external conditions.

Among other Dash 8 advances was a new traction alternator/rectifier design with power enough to supply both sufficient current for starting and sufficient voltage for high speeds without the need for electrical transition stages that matched alternator output with motor requirements.

The Dash 8 era began with experimental prototypes: a 3,600-horsepower four-axle designated B36-8 and a six-motor machine designated C39-8. Like other modern GE high-horsepower diesels, these were powered by the company's proven 16-cylinder FDL engine and the latest GE 752 traction motor. Rather than immediately supplant its proven Dash 7 line, GE strengthened its new technology by introducing a few small fleets of preproduction Dash 8 locomotives to be used by railroads in regular revenue service while serving as test beds for further development and encouraging railroad interest in the new product line. GE began mass production of the Dash 8 line in 1987, initially offering two models: the four-motor Dash 8-40B and the six-motor Dash 8-40C.

In 1989, the North American Safety Cab made its commercial debut. The transition to safety cab designs coincided with Dash 8 production. Mass-produced Dash 8-40CWs (*W* referring to the safety cab design that features a wider nose section) were first sold to Union Pacific in 1990. Within a few years most of GE's customers were purchasing locomotives with North American Safety Cabs, and only a few lines, such as Norfolk

Southern, continued to order the traditional cab design.

General Electric introduced its Dash 9 line in 1993. Compared with the Dash 8, which had implemented a variety of significant design changes, the Dash 9 was more of a marketing tool to distinguish smaller improvements that resulted in more capable locomotives and lower lifecycle costs. Innovations like electronic fuel injection and split cooling were first offered as options on late-era Dash 8s, but became standard features with the Dash 9 and would help GE meet more stringent air-quality requirements in the decade following the Dash 9's introduction. Other Dash 9 features included the high-adhesion HiAd truck and nominal external changes, such as a more ergonomic step and handrail arrangement to improve crew safety and comfort.

Far more significant than the Dash 9 was GE's first commercial alternating current traction locomotive. While both the DC-traction Dash 9 and the AC-traction AC4400CW are rated at 4,400 horsepower, AC traction was a major technological leap. Computer-controlled three-phase AC power substantially increased the tractive effort of an individual locomotive (allowing it to haul more tonnage) and improved dynamic braking capability while lowering electrical lifecycle costs.

Among the variations of this revolutionary locomotive were CSX's 500 series AC4400CWs, which are unusual in CSX's GE fleet because they carry an extra 10 tons of ballast to boost their tractive effort in slow-speed mineral service on very steep grades. In addition, CSX, Kansas City Southern, and CP Rail bought AC4400CWs with steerable GE trucks designed to reduce wheel and rail wear.

In the mid-1990s, GE introduced the AC6000CW as a high-horsepower competitor for EMD's SD90MAC-H, developed about the same time. Interest in this high-horsepower model stemmed in part from the cost advantages associated with unit reduction—one 6,000-horsepower diesel could replace a pair of 1970s-era EMD SD40-2s or GE C30-7s. To achieve this extreme horsepower, GE teamed with German engine manufacturer Deutz MWM in development of the 16-7HDL. This engine, like the long-established 16-7FDL, is a four-cycle design employing 16 cylinders in a 45-degree V configuration.

Among the striking features of the AC6000CW is a larger carbody and radiators with massive "wings" at the rear of the locomotive. Some AC6000CWs were "convertibles" built with the 4,400-horsepower 7FDL diesel, capable of a later upgrade to the more powerful engine. Only Union Pacific and CSX bought the AC6000CW, and the 6,000-horsepower concept fell out of favor before the model was built in large numbers. As a result, these big diesels remain among the more uncommon modern types.

Introduction of the Environmental Protection Agency's more stringent engine emissions requirements has played a significant role in recent GE locomotives. While GE was able to adapt its 7FDL engine to meet EPA Tier 0 and Tier 1 requirements, in order to comply with Tier 2 requirements that went into effect in 2005, GE engineered a new diesel engine, known as the GEVO, an evolutionary advancement of the FDL design. The GEVO was integral to introduction of GE's Evolution series, which can be ordered with either DC or AC traction, depending on intended application. As with the Dash 8s in the mid-1980s, in 2003 and 2004 GE built 50 preproduction locomotives for UP, BNSF, and NS, enabling GE to gain field experience with new configurations *before* it was required to meet Tier 2 standards in regular production.

Because few design changes were required, the preproduction units share a similar appearance with production Evolution units. The ES44AC and ES44DC remain GE's standard production models. A recent variation is the ES44C4, an AC-traction model that employs A1A trucks, allowing for a six-axle, four-motor model. This offers performance characteristics similar to DC traction Evolution locomotives, but provides some of the operating cost advantages of AC traction without the high price tag of a six-motor AC-traction model. In the future, the ES44C4 and similar models may result in the phasing out of GE's DC-traction line.

BNSF Dash 9-44CW leads an eastward double-stack along the Mississippi at Savanna, Illinois, on June 24, 2010. The Dash 9 employed variations of the 16-7FDL diesel and GE 752 traction motor, and it represents 30 years of engineering refinement. *Brian Solomon*

On July 8, 1994, leased LMX B39-8s bracket a cabless Burlington Northern B30-7A and lead an eastward intermodal train on the former Great Northern at Grizzly, Montana. The fleet of GE's LMX subsidiary represented the manufacturer's first full-service maintenance contract. GE serviced the locomotives at the old Chicago, Burlington & Quincy shops in Lincoln, Nebraska. *Brian Solomon*

An LMX B39-8 leads an eastward BN intermodal train on the Aurora Sub at Oregon, Illinois, on February 19, 1995. Except for three B32-8 preproduction prototypes, BN didn't operate Dash 8s dressed in its famous Cascade Green livery. *Brian Solomon*

New Conrail Dash 8-40B No. 5066 leads Chicago–Boston intermodal train TV14 at East Rochester, New York, on May 4, 1988. To convey the new line's higher quality, GE incorporated "Dash" into its new designations. While a clever marketing ploy, many railroads perpetuated the old classification system, which has resulted in confusion. *Brian Solomon*

In July 1989, Conrail B40-8 No. 5079 leads a westward intermodal upgrade on the old Pennsylvania Railroad at MG Tower. Conrail painted its Dash 8-40B fleet with a nose logo meant to represent a new era of cooperation between labor and management. *Brian Solomon*

In 1988, short-line operator New York, Susquehanna & Western bought four Dash 8-40Bs—built to Conrail specifications—for service on high-priority intermodal trains. In spring 1989, after NYS&W was designated operator of the bankrupt Delaware & Hudson, the railroad placed a second order that was backed by CSX. After D&H operations were conveyed to CP Rail in 1990, CSX took title of the second order. New B40-8 No. 4034 was seen at SK Yard in Buffalo, New York, on May 4, 1989. *Brian Solomon*

A warm morning on July 6, 1987, finds Conrail C32-8 No. 6613 and a pair of C30-7As leading eastward freight on the old Boston & Albany main line below the Massachusetts Turnpike at Woronoco. *Brian Solomon*

Norfolk Southern C39-8 No. 8669 leads a short Hanjin double-stack at Tifft Street in Buffalo, New York, in July 1989. When new, these NS locomotives were set up to run long hood forward. *Brian Solomon*

During Dash 8 development, GE built four fleets of prototypes for extensive road-service testing. Conrail tested 10 C32-8s (Nos. 6610–6619), unusual 3,250-horsepower six-motor models powered by the 12-cylinder FDL engine. On June 10, 1987, Conrail No. 6617 leads westward freight MBSE (Middleborough, Massachusetts, to Selkirk, New York) at West Brimfield, Massachusetts. *Brian Solomon*

General Electric's Dash 8-40C was a six-motor production model rated at 4,000 horsepower. Chicago & North Western No. 8548, with a westward, waits for a meet on April 22, 1995, just a few days before C&NW was officially absorbed into the Union Pacific system. *Brian Solomon*

Above: The Dash 8-40C was one of GE's biggest successes of the mid-1980s, reestablishing its reputation with railroads that had largely purchased EMD locomotives in the 1960s and 1970s and filling large orders with stalwart customers, such as CSX. On October 16, 2004, CSX Dash 8-40C No. 7530 and a former Conrail SD60 lead an eastward freight on the old West Shore Route at Guilderland, New York. *Brian Solomon*

Opposite: Conrail No. 6031 leads an excursion at Exchange Street in Buffalo, New York, on July 2, 1989. Difficulties with preserved Nickel Plate Road 2-8-4 No. 765 resulted in this rare use of a Dash 8-40C in passenger service. *Brian Solomon*

Above: Union Pacific Dash 8-40C No. 9335 works westward through Nevada's Clover Creek Canyon on March 3, 1997. Among the Dash 8 line's many advances was a powerful traction alternator/rectifier capable of supplying high voltage and high current to motors, and thus avoiding the need for complex motor transition circuitry that had been common on earlier models. *Brian Solomon*

Opposite top: A pair of Union Pacific Dash 8-40Cs leads an eastward grain train at Chappell, Nebraska, on September 26, 1989. *Brian Solomon*

Opposite bottom: Union Pacific Dash 8-40C No. 9184 races along in eastern Wyoming on September 26, 1989. The Dash 8 design used refined versions of GE's primary components: the successful FDL diesel engine and 752 series traction motors. Introduced with the Dash 8, the 752AG motor enabled GE to boost continuous tractive effort ratings by 5 to 11 percent over previous models. *Brian Solomon*

Former Santa Fe Dash 8-40BWs lead an eastward BNSF carload freight in eastern Colorado in September 1998. Although four-motor 500 series Dash 8-40BWs were bought for high-priority Super Fleet services, BNSF tended to assign the older four-motors to lower priority services as it acquired newer six-motor diesels. *Brian Solomon*

Among Santa Fe's hottest trains was Chicago–to–Richmond, California, symbol 199. On October 27, 1990, new Dash 8-40BW No. 513 leads 1-199-27 at McCook, Illinois, on the first leg of its westward journey. When new, Santa Fe's 500 series GEs were among the most intensively utilized locomotives in the United States. *Mike Abalos*

In April 1996, a pair of BNSF Dash 8-40BWs (also described as B40-8Ws) races westward on the old Chicago, Burlington & Quincy along the Mississippi River at Savanna, Illinois. *Brian Solomon*

Brand-new Santa Fe Dash 8-40CW No. 848 works west at Old Trojan on Ash Hill on June 12, 1992. Santa Fe's six-motor Dash 8s featured an unusual roof profile designed to accommodate dimensional constraints imposed by the coal-loading equipment at New Mexico's York Canyon mine. All Santa Fe 800 series locomotives, as well as many subsequent GE models, featured the nonstandard roof. *Brian Solomon*

Except for the North American Safety Cab, the Dash 8-40CW is essentially the same as the Dash 8-40C. Union Pacific No. 9475 works eastward with a K-Line double-stack east of Oxman, Oregon, on Encina Hill on July 12, 1993. *Brian Solomon*

A Union Pacific Dash 8-40CW works upgrade in the late afternoon at Paxton in California's Feather River Canyon on September 26, 1993. *Brian Solomon*

Conrail No. 6097 leads a westward freight near Mineral Point, Pennsylvania, on the old Pennsy main line on October 17, 1992. These locomotives were Conrail's first diesels with the North American Safety Cab (colloquially called the "widenose cab"), which has since become a standard feature on all new road freight diesels. The locomotive lacks ditch lights, now standard equipment that wasn't required when these locomotives were delivered in the early 1990s. *Brian Solomon*

Conrail Dash 8-40CW No. 6230, in fresh Conrail Quality paint, rolls west at Palmer, Massachusetts, on February 3, 1995. This rear view provides a good look at the Dash 8's radiator wings. In the 1990s, as GE increased engine output and was required to lower exhaust emissions, it increased the capacity of its radiator designs. The thinner radiator wings are an identifying feature of GE's older models. *Brian Solomon*

Conrail Dash 8-40CW No. 6118 leads eastward symbol freight BUOI (Buffalo, New York, to Oak Island, New Jersey) in deep snow on the former Erie Railroad at Rock Glen, New York, in January 1994. *Brian Solomon*

Right: This builder's plate was on a Chicago & North Western Dash 9-44CW constructed in April 1994. C&NW's Dash 9s were integrated into Union Pacific's fleet when UP absorbed the railroad in 1995. *Brian Solomon*

Below: A trio of new C&NW Dash 9-44CWs leads a Powder River Basin unit coal train through Creston, Illinois, on April 2, 1995. The Dash 9 era on C&NW was a short but colorful finale to the railroad's independent years. *Brian Solomon*

As a result of C&NW's unusual cab-signaling system, many of its former locomotives continued to work on former C&NW lines for several years after UP assumed control. On August 24, 1996, former C&NW Dash 9-44CW No. 8637 leads an eastward intermodal train on old home rails at Logan, Iowa. *Brian Solomon*

Designated Dash 9-44CWL, Canadian National's first Dash 9s were built in December 1994 (Nos. 2500–2522) and had a four-piece windshield instead of the two-piece design used in the United States. They were delivered with 70-mile-per-hour gearing but were limited to 65 miles per hour in Canada. This Dash 9 was photographed along the Mississippi River near Savanna, Illinois, on April 2, 1995. *Brian Solomon*

CN's later Dash 9s (Nos. 2523–2727), built as Dash 9-44CWs, use a variation of the two-piece windshield design. On June 14, 2004, No. 2680 leads a pair of EMD cowls northward at Lost Arrow Road in Byron, Wisconsin, on the former Wisconsin Central, which CN acquired in 2001. *Brian Solomon*

In 1994, Southern Pacific ordered Dash 9-44CWs that were assigned to a variety of heavy services, including iron ore trains operating from Minnesota's Iron Range to Geneva, Utah. In December 1994, a trio of new SP Dash 9s leads a taconite train on Wisconsin Central near Byron, Wisconsin. *Brian Solomon*

On September 11, 1994, a recently delivered Santa Fe Dash 9-44CW (known to the railroad as a C44-9W) leads a Union Equity unit train full of Kansas wheat on Santa Fe's Galveston Subdivision at Rosenburg, Texas. As in the case with Santa Fe's earlier six-motor safety cabs, their Dash 9s featured a distinctive cab roof profile. *Tom Kline*

New BNSF Dash 9-44CWs lead symbol freight S-CHIRIC (Stack–Chicago to Richmond, California) westward at Sugar Creek, Missouri, in August 1997. For almost two years after the 1995 BNSF merger, the new railroad continued to order a portion of its new power in Super Fleet paint, a variation of the scheme designed in the 1930s for Electro-Motive diesels built for the streamlined *Super Chief*. *Chris Guss*

Among the features made standard with the Dash 9 model was GE's new HiAd truck design, as seen on this new Santa Fe unit in 1994. *Brian Solomon*

BNSF Dash 9-44CWs lead a westward freight through the Feather River Canyon near Rich Bar, California, on August 15, 2009. *Brian Solomon*

This going-away view of the same train pictured on the facing page shows four BNSF Dash 9-44CWs approaching Rich Bar, California, with a long carload freight that originated at Pasco, Washington. At the back of this train are two additional Dash 9-44CWs working as distributed power units (DPUs), remotely controlled via radio from the head end. *Brian Solomon*

Dwarfed by massive basalt cliffs, a pair of BNSF Dash 9-44CWs leads an eastward unit grain train winding along Washington's Columbia River Gorge near Cooks Point on September 24, 2004. *Tom Kline*

Norfolk Southern was the only American railroad to order Dash 9s with a conventional cab—essentially the body style introduced with the older Dash models in the mid-1980s. In October 2001, NS No. 8771 leads an eastward intermodal train on the former Erie Railroad main line near Waverly, New York. *Brian Solomon*

Above and opposite: Norfolk Southern Dash 9-40C No. 8782 rolls eastward through Roanoke, Virginia, in October 2005. Like NS's Dash 9-40CW, the Dash 9-40C is rated at just 4,000 horsepower rather than 4,400 horsepower. By lowering the maximum output in the higher throttle notches, NS can better conserve fuel. *Brian Solomon*

A Norfolk Southern Dash 9-40CW races eastward on the old Pennsy main line near Mexico, Pennsylvania. NS Dash 9-40CWs use the same frame, HiAd trucks, 16-cylinder 7FDL engine, and 752AH-31 traction motors as the Dash 9-44CW. However, software in the locomotive's engine-governing unit rates the locomotive at 4,000 horsepower rather than the more common 4,400 horsepower. *Brian Solomon*

On July 19, 2009, NS Dash 9-40CW No. 9575 leads eastward unit coal train No. 532 on the former Erie Railroad main line east of Alfred, New York. NS sends coal trains and empties over the former Erie route between Meadville, Pennsylvania, and Hornell, New York. The section was closed to through traffic during the Conrail era, but was reopened in 2003 by short-line operator Western New York & Pennsylvania. *Brian Solomon*

This view of NS Dash 9-40CW No. 9764 at Roanoke, Virginia, offers a good look at the top of the cab and hood. Notice the second locomotive is painted only in primer. Later, after the locomotive entered service, it was given a fresh coat of NS paint. *Brian Solomon*

On July 20, 1995, against the backdrop of the Book Cliffs, a pair of new Southern Pacific AC4400CWs leads a unit taconite train west on the former Denver & Rio Grande Western main line in the Utah desert near Solitude. *Brian Solomon*

On July 18, 1995, a trio of new SP AC4400CWs leads an eastward unit coal train out of the tunnels at Kyune, Utah, on the former D&RGW/Utah Railway crossing of Soldier Summit. *Brian Solomon*

SP AC4400CW No. 101 eases a loaded taconite train downgrade through the Deen Tunnel near Pando, Colorado, on the former D&RGW crossing of Tennessee Pass. The line over the pass was among the steepest and highest in the United States before Union Pacific closed it in 1997. Freight movement over this route benefited only briefly from modern AC-traction diesels like this. *Brian Solomon*

Shortly before being absorbed by Union Pacific in spring 1995, Chicago & North Western took delivery of its last new locomotives: AC4400CWs that it assigned to Powder River Basin coal trains. C&NW No. 8810 is at Bill, Wyoming, in May 1995. Externally, the AC4400CW looks similar to the DC-traction Dash 9-44CW, except for the extended electrical cabinets housing the AC inverters behind the cab on the fireman's side. *Brian Solomon*

On the clear morning of July 12, 2005, Union Pacific AC4400CW No. 5922 leads a pair of EMD SD9043MACs eastbound at Troy, California, toward the famous Donner Summit on the old Southern Pacific. *Brian Solomon*

UP assigns its own locomotive model classifications, which often differ from the manufacturers' designations. According to UP, No. 5767 is a C44AC-CTE. The last three letters denote "controlled tractive effort," a feature that reduces maximum tractive effort for specific applications, such as work as DPUs. *Brian Solomon*

Above: CSX's 500 series AC4400CWs have an extra 10 tons of ballast to boost their tractive effort in slow-speed heavy service. Although originally assigned to coal trains on the old Baltimore & Ohio, in recent years 500 series AC4400CWs have been routinely assigned to service on the Boston Line in Massachusetts. No. 580 was photographed in fresh paint at Worcester, Massachusetts. *Brian Solomon*

Opposite top: At 11:36 a.m. on October 14, 2006, CSX Q116 drifts downgrade on the old Boston & Albany main line east of Becket, Massachusetts, at the Twin Ledges. No. 558 is one of CSX's heavy AC4400CWs featuring extra ballast. The trailing AC6000CW illustrates the difference in radiator profiles between the two diesels. *Brian Solomon*

Opposite bottom: CSX AC4400CW No. 588 and SD70MAC No. 4723 work west on the old West Shore Route across the bridge at French's Hollow, New York, on May 29, 2004. CSX identifies its AC-traction diesels with a lightning bolt below the road number. *Brian Solomon*

Kansas City Southern AC4400CWs Nos. 2011 and 2039 lead a southward grain train at Butlers Bluff, Missouri, on March 21, 2004. These AC4400CWs feature GE's steerable trucks, offered as an option in later years. Steerable trucks reduce friction in curves, thus minimizing wheel and rail wear while improving adhesion and fuel economy. The arrival of these locomotives in 1999 with distributed power capability brought an end to two of KCS's longstanding manned helper districts. *Chris Guss*

BNSF acquired a nominal fleet of production-built AC4400CWs before participating in GE's effort to advance the Evolution design. Built in late 2003 and early 2004, BNSF's prototypes were designated AC4400CWs and classed AC4400EV by BNSF. These were successful and BNSF ordered more than 600 production ES44ACs. *Chris Guss*

CP Rail AC4400CW No. 9635 works west with a loaded grain train near Lake Louise, Alberta, in August 1998. This is the typical power setup for CP Rail bulk trains operating in western Canada: two AC-traction locomotives on the head end and a third positioned approximately two-thirds back in the train. *Chris Guss*

In the mid-1990s Union Pacific ordered a fleet of locomotives from GE featuring the larger platform designed for the 6,000-horsepower AC6000CW but delivered with the older 4,400-horsepower 7FDL engine. UP later received a small fleet of true AC6000CWs powered by the 7HDL diesel, but the so-called "convertible" locomotives remained 4,400-horsepower machines and were known on the railroad as C6044ACs. *Brian Solomon*

A CSX AC6000CW works eastward through the Quaboag River Valley near West Warren, Massachusetts, on the former Boston & Albany main line. *Brian Solomon*

Opposite bottom: CSX bought the largest fleet of AC6000CWs. GE licensed design elements from German firm Deutz MWM, which were incorporated into the new four-cycle 7HDL. *Brian Solomon*

CSX No. 1, a GE AC4400CW, leads a loaded coal drag at the 21 Bridge east of Keyser, West Virginia, on October 17, 2002. Since buying its first AC4400CWs, CSX has assembled one of the largest fleets of AC-traction diesels in the United States. *Brian Solomon*

A rolling meet on the old Boston & Albany at milepost 130 finds CSX AC6000CW No. 689 leading an eastward train while brand-new ES44DCs work upgrade with Q119 (Boston to Chicago). Today, CSX operates a variety of modern GE six-motor diesels in heavy mainline service. *Brian Solomon*

On May 20, 2004, CSX AC4400CW No. 590 restrains an eastward train descending the Boston & Albany route near milepost 130. Improved dynamic braking is among the advantages offered by modern AC traction. *Brian Solomon*

BNSF is one of several American railroads to order separate fleets of AC- and DC-traction GE Evolution series locomotives. Externally, the locomotives appear almost the same, but their intended applications are distinct: AC locomotives are assigned to heavy service, such as coal trains, while DC locomotives are assigned to manifest and intermodal services. BNSF ES44DC No. 7649 leads an eastward freight on the former Western Pacific at Keddie, California, on August 15, 2009. *Brian Solomon*

This eastward CSX freight near Syracuse, Indiana, on June 14, 2010, provides a contrast in modern GE DC-traction diesels. Leading is CSX No. 5401, an ES44DC built new in 2007; trailing is a 1980s-era Dash 8-40C, among GE's first mass-produced microprocessor-controlled models. *Brian Solomon*

Canadian National ES44DC No. 2241 leads a pair of 1990s-era Dash 9-44CWs on the old Wisconsin Central just south of the Wisconsin–Illinois state line on June 15, 2010. CN has equipped its ES44DCs with distributed power and recently has expanded the use of this technology to include both older GEs and EMD SD70M-2s. *Brian Solomon*

Norfolk Southern ES40DC No. 7505 leads an empty hopper train west at Roanoke, Virginia, in October 2005. Like NS's Dash 9-40CWs, the railroad's Evolution series locomotives are rated at 4,000 horsepower rather than 4,400 to help conserve fuel. The change in output is accomplished electronically; mechanically, the two models are essentially the same. *Brian Solomon*

NS ES40DC No. 7505 was among the Evolution series prototypes built at Erie, Pennsylvania, in 2004, when the 1990s-era AC4400CW and Dash 9 models were still in regular production for domestic applications. The Evolution series supplanted the 1990s-era models when they entered full production in 2005. *Brian Solomon*

Norfolk Southern No. 7649 leads empty hopper train No. 691 westward on the former Pennsy Middle Division at Mexico, Pennsylvania, at 5:03 p.m. on July 1, 2010. This was one of 220 ES40DCs on the NS roster in July 2010. NS also has a fleet of 24 ES44ACs purchased in 2008 (Nos. 8000–8023). *Brian Solomon*

In May 2007, brand-new CSX ES44DC No. 5412 and AC4400CW No. 101 are down to a crawl with a heavy train of building debris on the former Boston & Albany west of Chester, Massachusetts. In October 2009, CSX started down-rating its ES44DCs to 4,000 horsepower and redesignating them ES40DCs. *Brian Solomon*

Above: CSX ES44DC No. 5211 is factory-fresh in this October 2, 2005, view at Stony Creek, Virginia, on the former Atlantic Coast Line main line. Trailing is another new Evolution series locomotive still wearing gray primer. *Brian Solomon*

Opposite: Among the distinct identifying characteristics of the Evolution series is the profile of extra-large radiator wings at the back of the locomotives. The Evolution series radiator package includes a state-of-the-art air-to-air heat exchanger and dual fans that allow the intercooler to lower engine gas emissions and extend life. *Brian Solomon*

BNSF ES44DC No. 7759 was only a few weeks out of GE's Erie, Pennsylvania, plant when it was photographed at Silo, New Mexico, on September 26, 2005. BNSF has ordered both AC and DC Evolutions for different applications; however, the success of the four-motor, six-axle ES44C4 may have the railroad focusing on AC types for future acquisitions. *Tom Kline*

Above: A BNSF westward freight works upgrade on the former Denver & Rio Grande Western at Thompson, Utah, on June 12, 2009. When Union Pacific absorbed Southern Pacific in 1996, BNSF acquired trackage rights on portions of the old D&RGW to maintain the guise of rail competition in the Central Corridor. BNSF No. 7284 was part of an order for 148 ES44DCs completed in the first three quarters of 2009. *Philip A. Brahms*

Opposite: On February 24, 2010, new BNSF Railway ES44DC No. 7297 leads a westward autorack train on the former Santa Fe at Collier, California. Notice the difference in the cab profile between the Evolution series, which has a standard GE cab roof, and the Dash 9s trailing behind with the specially designed cab roof specified by Santa Fe. *Philip A. Brahms*

Above: This rear view of BNSF ES44AC No. 5922 at Milano, Texas, offers an excellent perspective of the locomotive's HiAd trucks, 5,000-gallon fuel tanks, and extra-large radiator, which characterize the heavy appearance of the Evolution series. The defining equipment of the Evolution series, however, is concealed under the hood: GE's powerful and Tier II emissions-compliant GEVO-12 diesel engine. *Tom Kline*

Opposite: On August 15, 2009, new BNSF ES44ACs in fresh paint work west of Ottumwa, Iowa, with an intermodal train on the former Chicago, Burlington & Quincy main line. BNSF tends to send new coal power west from Chicago in groups like this. Once at Lincoln or Alliance, Nebraska, they can be placed in coal service. *Chris Guss*

The AC Motors decal applied to the HiAd truck on BNSF ES44AC No. 5921 is a reminder to shop forces accustomed to the common DC-traction motors on most of the fleet. GE offers its Evolution series in both AC- and DC-traction varieties. GE specs indicate that the ES44AC delivers 198,000 pounds of starting tractive effort compared to just 142,000 pounds on the ES44DC. The ES44AC can maintain 166,000 pounds of continuous tractive effort at very slow speeds; the ES44DC offers 109,000 pounds. *Tom Kline*

CP Rail ES44AC No. 8743 leads a southward freight on the old Delaware & Hudson at East Worcester, New York, on October 10, 2007. Since 2005, CP Rail has focused new locomotive acquisitions on the Evolution series AC-traction model. These are numbered in the 8700 and 8800 series and assigned to mainline freight services. *Brian Solomon*

Between Toronto, Ontario, and Binghamton, New York, CP traffic and locomotives run through as train Nos. 254 eastbound/255 westbound. On Norfolk Southern's former Erie Railroad trackage east of Buffalo, the trains operate with NS crews and carry NS symbols 38T eastbound/39T westbound. On February 11, 2010, ES44AC No. 8767 stirs up fresh powder at Dalton, New York, as it roars down the old Erie Railroad with 38T in tow. *Brian Solomon*

CP Rail ES44AC No. 8757 and an AC4400CW lead eastward train No. 198 on the former Milwaukee Road main line at Wepco, Wisconsin. Once famous for the fast-running *Hiawatha*, this route is now CP Rail's main line from western Canada and the Twin Cities to Chicago. While AC-traction locomotives really aren't needed in this flat terrain, CP prefers the flexibility of assigning its road units anywhere they're needed. *Chris Guss*

CSX empty autorack train Q293 climbs west on Washington Hill through pastoral scenery near Middlefield, Massachusetts, on October 17, 2009. ES44AC No. 945 was one of an order for 50 such locomotives in CSX's 900 series. Where CSX's ES44DCs are numbered in the 5200–5500 series, the AC-traction models carry three-digit numbers in the 700–900 series. *Brian Solomon*

CSX's ES44ACs feature steerable trucks instead of the more common GE HiAd trucks ordered on most new Evolution series locomotives. A variety of CSX AC-traction diesels have used the steerable truck, including its AC6000CW fleet and some of its AC4400CWs. *Brian Solomon*

Two CSX ES44ACs equipped with distributed power lead southbound utility coal across the Copper Creek Viaduct on the former Clinchfield near Speers Ferry, Virginia. A third ES44AC will be added to the rear of this train at Erwin, Tennessee, and linked via radio telemetry to operate as a remote locomotive. Operation of loaded coal trains with distributed power on the single-track former Clinchfield has eliminated a manned helper district and provided needed capacity to operate additional trains. *T. S. Hoover*

Above: Union Pacific ES44AC No. 5455 leads autoracks westward on the old Southern Pacific at Pinole, California, on August 26, 2009. UP, which doesn't employ GE's model designations, classifies this locomotive as a C45ACCTE. *Brian Solomon*

Opposite bottom: No. 2010, an experimental Evolution series hybrid, was displayed at Chicago on September 16, 2008. GE hopes to engineer modern hybrid technology using onboard batteries to store surplus energy generated during dynamic braking. While the technology is new, the concept is not: In the late 1920s GE built "tri-power" electric-diesels with banks of storage batteries, primarily for service on New York Central's electrified territory in New York City. *Chris Guss*

UP ES44AC No. 2010 was specially painted to commemorate the Boy Scouts of America centennial. It features the BSA logo on the side of the cab and merit badges on the walkway. The locomotive was photographed at an unveiling ceremony in Houston, Texas, on March 10, 2010, home to the largest troop council in the United States. *Tom Kline*

Today it's standard on the Union Pacific to operate locomotives as distributed power units. Radio-controlled DPU locomotives may be situated in the middle of a consist or at the back, reducing drawbar stress, lowering fuel consumption, improving train control, and eliminating most manned helper districts. On July 31, 2009, ES44AC No. 7918 leads a stack train on the former Western Pacific at Jungo, Nevada. Another ES44AC working as a DPU is situated at the rear of the train. *Brian Solomon*

Above: In the early morning of August 15, 2009, UP ES44AC No. 7635 leads a westward double-stack through the Feather River Canyon west of Virgilia, California. Forest fires burning in the Sierra filled the atmosphere with smoke and ash, lending an unusually rosy and dusty quality to the light. *Brian Solomon*

Opposite bottom: UP ES44AC No. 7412 catches the evening sun while working as a DPU at the back of a westward double-stack descending the former Western Pacific grade near Elsie, California, on August 14, 2009. *Brian Solomon*

Iowa Interstate Railroad (IAIS) ES44AC No. 512 bucks snow east of McClelland, Iowa, on the old Rock Island Chicago–Omaha main line. Unlike many smaller freight carriers that relied exclusively on second-hand locomotives, Iowa Interstate made the bold decision to purchase 12 state-of-the-art AC-traction Evolution series diesels to accommodate growing ethanol traffic. These were delivered in late 2008; in 2009, Iowa Interstate acquired two more units that were originally ordered by CSX. *Chris Guss*

Rock Island was liquidated in 1980, a decade before modern wide cabs were introduced, but this specially painted IAIS ES44AC leading a unit ethanol train at New Lenox, Illinois, in January 2010, offers a vision of what a modern Rock Island locomotive might have looked like. *Marshall W. Beecher*

IAIS acknowledges its Rock Island heritage by adapting the Rock Island herald. While many railroads have painted locomotives in heritage colors, in recent years only Iowa Interstate, Union Pacific, and Kansas City Southern have applied traditional paint to brand-new power.
Chris Guss

The ES44C4 is a six-axle, four-motor variation of the Evolution series. GE's locomotive test car divides a consist of four BNSF ES44C4s during a performance demonstration at Steward, Illinois, on March 12, 2009. The ES44C4 offers tractive and braking effort equivalent to a six-axle DC-propulsion locomotive while using four AC-traction motors on the number one, three, four, and six axles. AC-traction motors are more reliable and require less maintenance than the DC motors they replace. *Terry Norton*

The last light of October 29, 2008, paints the flanks of two Norfolk Southern ES44ACs pushing utility coal train No. 756 up the Elkhorn Grade at Elkhorn, West Virginia. NS's 24 NS ES44ACs feature additional ballast weight and, according to GE, have the greatest tractive and dynamic braking efforts of any commercially built diesel-electric locomotive. Because of this, they are ideally suited for helper assignments on the difficult grades of the Pocahontas Division. *T. S. Hoover*

One advantage of AC-traction systems is the ability to deliver substantially higher tractive effort. On November 6, 2008, a pair of nearly new NS ES44ACs working at full power assist utility coal train No. 762 in its ascent of the Elkhorn Grade on the former Norfolk & Western at Switchback, West Virginia. Since their arrival on the NS in 2008, pairs of ES44ACs have replaced sets of three DC six-axle locomotives as manned helper consists on the Pocahontas Division in Virginia and West Virginia. *T. S. Hoover*

Chapter 2

Electro-Motive Division

Electro-Motive Division

In the 1970s, General Motors' Electro-Motive Division reigned as North America's leading locomotive manufacturer, a position it had held since the late 1940s. By the late 1970s, concerns with rising fuel costs, and greater fuel efficiency offered by General Electric's 7FDL engine, encouraged EMD to push its technology to new limits. While the 16-645E3 engine used to power its GP40-2 and SD40-2 locomotives had been rated at 3,000 horsepower, its new 16-645F3 engine was rated at 3,500 horsepower. To more effectively apply the increased output, EMD developed an improved wheel-slip control system called Super Series intended to boost wheel-rail adhesion. After producing a few experimental GP40Xs and SD40Xs that incorporated elements of its new technology, EMD introduced the 3,500-horsepower GP50 and SD50 production models (50 series) in 1981. (Horsepower was increased to 3,600 on later versions.) In addition to the new engine, these models employed the latest generation of electrical components. At 71 feet 2 inches, the SD50 was significantly longer than the SD40-2 that it supplanted as the builder's standard six-motor freight diesel.

Unfortunately, difficulties developed with locomotives powered by 16-645F engines. EMD refined a new engine block and developed an improved line of locomotives, known as its 60 series, using the new 710G engine derived from the 645 design, along with an improved electrical system incorporating microprocessors. In 1984, it began production of the six-motor 3,800-horsepower SD60, followed by the four-motor GP60 in 1985. The production of 50 series and 60 series locomotives overlapped by a couple of years while EMD perfected its new designs; externally, comparable models from the two series were similar in appearance.

Between 1987 and 1992, Electro-Motive implemented fundamental changes to its manufacturing process that resulted in the shifting of locomotive assembly for domestic sales from its La Grange, Illinois, plant to its London, Ontario–based Diesel Division. (In addition, some locomotive assembly was undertaken at other locations, including Conrail's Juniata Shops at Altoona, Pennsylvania, and at Super Steel in Schenectady, New York.)

Another change for EMD was the introduction and adoption of the modern

North American Safety Cab. Adapted from a Canadian cab design, the first application of the new cab style in the United States was on an order for Union Pacific SD60Ms that entered service during the early part of 1989. Initially, the SD60M used the safety cab configuration with a three-piece windshield as had been used for Canadian freight locomotives and the F59PH passenger diesel. Later locomotives utilized a refined design with a slightly tapered cab and a two-piece windshield. During the 1990s, EMD's safety cab design evolved. One variation was the whisper cab, sometimes referred to as an isolated cab because of its design that isolated the cab frame from the underframe superstructure. By the early 1990s, most railroads had adopted the safety cab, which has since become standard on all new freight locomotives.

In the 1990s, EMD introduced new locomotive lines for heavy-freight service. Its SD70 series made its debut in late 1992. The 4,000-horsepower SD70M represented a refinement of existing technology rather than a major change to primary components. By contrast, the SD70MAC, which made its debut a year later, ushered in a fundamental change in locomotive design. This was America's first commercially successful, heavy-haul diesel using a state-of-the-art three-phase alternating current traction system. Developed with German manufacturer Siemens, this system was applied experimentally to a pair of F69PHACs demonstrated on Amtrak in the early 1990s and then on four SD60MACs tested on Burlington Northern. BN was EMD's first major customer for AC traction. Superior traction characteristics allowed BN to assign three 4,000-horsepower SD70MAC units in place of five conventional 3,000-horsepower DC-traction units in Powder River coal service in Wyoming.

EMD continued to offer DC-traction models and sold several variations of its SD70, including the aforementioned SD70M, a conventional-cab model designated simply as an SD70 (bought by Norfolk Southern and Illinois Central), a whisper cab model SD70I, and uprated 4,300-horsepower variations designated SD75M and SD75I to Santa Fe/BNSF and Canadian National, respectively.

In the mid-1990s, EMD engineered its 6,000-horsepower SD90MAC-H and a convertible variation often known as an SD9043MAC (in effect, an SD70MAC capable of being upgraded to SD90MAC-H specs). Significantly, for the 6,000-horsepower model, EMD needed to develop an entirely new diesel engine, the four-cycle 265H, in order to generate 6,000 horsepower.

In the past decade, Electro-Motive engineered improvements to its locomotive line to comply with EPA emissions standards.

Reflecting these changes, it brought out its latest freight diesels in 2005: the DC-traction SD70M-2 and AC-traction SD70ACe. Also in that year, General Motors sold EMD to a consortium of Greenbriar Equity and Berkshire Partners. The initials EMD today stand for Electro-Motive Diesel. In 2010, EMD changed ownership again when it was sold to Caterpillar subsidiary Progress Rail Services. The company continues to manufacture its SD70M-2/SD70ACe lines, models that are virtually indistinguishable on the outside but have different performance characteristics—and different price tags.

Two Conrail SD80MACs, Nos. 4127 and 4116, glide eastward with autorack train ML-482 at Muddy Pond just east of Washington Summit near Hinsdale, Massachusetts. *Brian Solomon*

Above: Vermont Railway briefly operated two GP60s built for the Texas-Mexican Railway. On February 18, 2002, train No. 263, running from Rutland to Bellows Falls, Vermont, has freshly painted GP60 No. 381 in the lead as it ascends the grade to Mount Holly. *Brian Solomon*

Opposite top: Burlington Northern GP50 No. 3141 leads a westward intermodal train at East Dubuque, Illinois, in June 1995. The GP50 was the successor to the very popular GP40/GP40-2. Rated at 3,500 horsepower, it was powered by the 16-645F engine. Few railroads bought GP50s, and only a handful remain active in mainline service. *Brian Solomon*

Opposite bottom: Among EMD's more unusual modern four-axle models was the GP59, which only Norfolk Southern bought new. On October 17, 2008, NS No. 4616 works local freight H2R on the former Erie Railroad at Silver Springs, New York. Similar in appearance to the more common GP60, the GP59 was intended for high-horsepower applications and powered by a fuel-efficient 12-cylinder 710G engine rated at 3,000 horsepower compared with the GP60's 3,800 horsepower. *Brian Solomon*

Above: Southern Pacific GP60 No. 9746 leads a westward intermodal train destined for Oakland along the shores of San Pablo Bay at Pinole, California. SP was the largest buyer of the GP60, acquiring nearly 200 units for itself and its Cotton Belt and Denver & Rio Grande Western affiliates. *Brian Solomon*

Opposite top: SP's last new four-motor diesels were 25 3,800-horsepower GP60s built between November 1993 and January 1994. Photographed at Wendel, California, on February 11, 1994, No. 9789 was only weeks old. It was assigned to work a manifest freight on the remote Modoc Line between Klamath Falls, Oregon, and a connection with Union Pacific's former Western Pacific line at Flannigan, Nevada. *Brian Solomon*

This is a Blomberg truck on SP No. 9789. SP's GP60s used 70:17 gearing for fast intermodal work. Typical EMD road locomotives built between the 1970s and early 1990s used 62:18 gearing designed for a maximum operating speed of 65 miles per hour. By the time SP received its last GP60s, high-horsepower six-motor diesels were standard road freight locomotives in North America. *Brian Solomon*

Norfolk Southern SD50 No. 6522 leads eastward intermodal No. 168 on CP Rail's Delaware & Hudson route at Nineveh, New York, on October 13, 2003. This SD50 wasn't making points with the railroad; it wasn't loading properly and as a result the train stalled climbing Belden Hill out of Binghamton, New York. A following CP Rail train shoved 168 to the top of the hill and from that point on a trailing NS GE-built Dash 9-40CW moved 168 eastward to Albany. *Brian Solomon*

Canadian National bought a cowl body type variation of the SD50 designated SD50F. Sixty were built by EMD affiliate GMD at London, Ontario, between 1985 and 1987. Like other late-era SD50s, they were powered by the 16-645F3B engine rated at 3,600 horsepower and geared for 65 miles per hour. No. 5434 leads a southward freight on the former Wisconsin Central near Church Road in Byron, Wisconsin, on June 22, 2004. *Brian Solomon*

The SD50 resulted from EMD's efforts to improve upon its popular 1970s-era SD40-2. Regular production began in 1981, and the design was originally rated at 3,500 horsepower; later production SD50s were upped to 3,600 horsepower. All were powered by the 16-645F diesel and used state-of-the-art D87 traction motors. Due to perceived design flaws, the locomotives have been compared unfavorably with the SD40-2. On June 28, 1996, Union Pacific No. 5011 leads Conrail empty hopper train UNW-417 on Conrail trackage at Hammond, Indiana. *Mike Abalos*

Opposite top: Norfolk Southern SD40Es shove a loaded unit coal train toward the summit of the Alleghenies at Gallitzin, Pennsylvania, on June 30, 2010. The SD40E designation for NS's rebuilt 1980s-era SD50s reflects the work done to them, with the "E" inferring "enhanced" and describing the modern electrical system that provides greater tractive effort than available from a conventional SD40-2. NS evaluated eight microprocessor controls before choosing EMD's EM2000 system. *Brian Solomon*

Opposite bottom: One of CSX's rebuilt SD50 models—SD50-3 No. 8526—works eastward on the former Baltimore & Ohio main line near Nappanee, Indiana, on June 14, 2010. CSX's constituent railroads, Chessie System and Seaboard System, placed significant orders for SD50s in the mid-1980s. *Brian Solomon*

Right: On July 1, 2010, a pair of NS SD40Es shoves on the back of a heavy westward freight at Gallitzin, Pennsylvania. NS has rebuilt a number of former Conrail SD50s, as SD40Es, downgrading the 3,500-horsepower 16-645F engine to a 3,000-horsepower 16-645E3C configuration and replacing the electrical system with modern microprocessor controls. In 2010, the rebuilding program was still underway and expected to result in a 54-unit fleet of manned helpers. *Brian Solomon*

Above: An SD60 leads a Norfolk Southern RoadRailer westward on the old Wabash near Attica, Indiana, on October 20, 2002. The SD60 was an improvement on the SD50, employing the new 16-710G engine and microprocessor controls. Variations of the SD60 include the SD60M with a North American Safety Cab, the SD60I with an isolated cab to reduce noise, and Canadian National's SD60F with a cowl body style. *Brian Solomon*

Opposite top: On September 20, 1989, new Conrail SD60s work west with train TV201X, carrying K-Line containers on the former New York Central Water Level Route at Dunkirk, New York. Computer controls in the 60 series diesel allowed more precise regulation of engine and electrical components, controlled main generator excitation, and provided detailed computerized diagnostic systems for more effective analysis of performance flaws. *Brian Solomon*

On July 12, 1994, Oakway SD60 No. 9002 works an empty coal train westward on Burlington Northern's former Northern Pacific main line near Sentinel Butte in the North Dakota Badlands. Oakway provided BN with a "power by the hour" fleet of 100 SD60s. *Brian Solomon*

Burlington Northern SD60Ms lead an eastward CP Rail freight on the former Milwaukee Road just south of downtown Milwaukee, Wisconsin, on July 8, 1995. No. 9254 is representative of later SD60Ms that featured a two-piece windshield and a slightly tapered nose section. The early SD60Ms had an untapered, boxier nose and a three-piece windshield. *Brian Solomon*

On July 27, 1991, Union Pacific SD60M No. 6255 leads a westward freight upgrade on Encina Hill near Oxman, Oregon. Two SD40-2s work as manned helpers at the back. UP's first SD60Ms entered service in early 1989, 20 years after UP's famous DDA40X Centennials, which featured the 1960s version of a wide-nose cab. *Brian Solomon*

On May 22, 1993, UP SD60M No. 6172 works eastward through the Feather River Canyon on the former Western Pacific main line. Known in some circles as "Cyclops" for their distinctive appearance, SD60Ms were commonly assigned to lead UP freights on this route in the early 1990s. *Brian Solomon*

Conrail SD60I leads intermodal train TV6 eastward at the Twin Ledges east of Becket, Massachusetts, at 10:03 a.m. on May 24, 1997. Conrail operated both SD60Ms and SD60Is. The latter featured the noise-reducing whisper cab (a.k.a. isolated cab) and was assembled at the railroad's Juniata Shops in Altoona, Pennsylvania. *Brian Solomon*

On July 1, 2010, three former Conrail SD60Is leading westward coal-hopper train No. 643 at Cassandra, Pennsylvania, descend the western slope of the former Pennsylvania Railroad's Allegheny crossing. Because of tight clearances on the rotary car dumper at Pennsylvania Power & Light's Strawberry Ridge power plant, dedicated locomotives are assigned to Norfolk Southern's PP&L unit trains. In recent years the railroad has used SD60Is in three-unit sets. *Brian Solomon*

On February 20, 2004, CSX SD60I No. 8731 rolls across the trestle at Weldon, North Carolina, on the former Atlantic Coast Line main line. This angle offers a view of the metal separating the cab and the front of the locomotive nose, which is an identifying feature of EMD's whisper cab and distinguishes the SD60M from the SD60I. *Brian Solomon*

On May 27, 1991, five GP60Ms lead hot Santa Fe intermodal No. 1-198-27 at McCook, Illinois. Six-motor units with North American Safety Cabs became standard on U.S. main lines in the 1990s, but only Santa Fe ordered modern four-motor units with this cab design for high-speed intermodal service. The GP60M and cabless GP60B were unique to Santa Fe and, after 1995, Santa Fe's successor, BNSF. *Mike Abalos*

In October 1990, a nearly new Santa Fe GP60M leads a westward intermodal train through California's Glen Frazer Canyon. The high-horsepower four-motor diesels were standard power on trains to and from Richmond, California. *Brian Solomon*

A trio of Santa Fe GP60Ms races eastward with a stack train in New Mexico in January 1994. In the late 1980s, Santa Fe worked with GM and GE to design the North American Safety Cab as part of its concessions to reduce crew sizes and lengthen crew districts. The new cab had its origins in designs used by Canadian lines and was intended to reduce engine noise; provide desktop controls, giving the engineer a forward-facing position; and provide greater structural safety in the event of a collision. *Brian Solomon*

In the 1990s, Illinois Central bucked the trends toward AC traction, North American Safety Cabs, and other innovations by ordering very basic SD70s. A pair of these race northward on IC's main line in central Illinois on June 23, 2004. By then, IC was part of the Canadian National system. *Brian Solomon*

IC received 40 SD70s from EMD in 1995 (Nos. 1000–1039). It was one of just three railroads to receive this conventional-cab model. The class leader was on display at Homewood, Illinois, in October 1995. *Brian Solomon*

Illinois Central SD70 No. 1008 basks in the glow of sodium vapor lights reflecting off snow at Genoa, Illinois. Powered by EMD's successful 16-710G3B engine, the SD70 was rated at 4,000 horsepower. Only 120 conventional-cab SD70s were built, making them rare among the more than 1,600 SD70 series locomotives built with variations of the North American Safety Cab. *Chris Guss*

Above: In May 2002, Norfolk Southern SD70s Nos. 2578 and 2582 are virtually spotless as they approach South Fork, Pennsylvania, with a five-car company business train. *Brian Solomon*

Opposite bottom: Conrail's last locomotives were ordered by its new owners, CSX and Norfolk Southern, but delivered in Conrail paint. The 2500 series SD70s were built to NS specifications, including a conventional cab and control stand. By contrast, CSX ordered SD70MACs. Here, new Conrail SD70s work west between Spruce Creek and Union Furnace, Pennsylvania, in November 1998. Six months later this route became part of the NS system. *Brian Solomon*

NS SD70 No. 2561 leads an empty Mount Tom coal train westward on Guilford Rail System's Boston & Maine route at Eagle Bridge, New York, in October 2001. *Brian Solomon*

SD70M demonstrators made their rounds on Southern Pacific in June 1993, painted in EMD's latest demonstrator scheme. The primary difference between the SD70M and the SD70 was the cab style. *Brian Solomon*

SP's last new EMDs—and its only EMDs with North American Safety Cabs—were 25 units purchased in 1994. Initially, many of these were assigned to work between Portland, Oregon, and Los Angeles on the so-called I-5 Corridor. In June 1994, new SP No. 9808 was photographed on a freight in Loring, Kansas, on Union Pacific trackage rights. In Topeka, the train would switch to home rails for the trip west. *Chris Guss*

Norfolk Southern operates several variations of the SD70, including conventional-cab SD70s, early- and late-era SD70Ms, and the more modern SD70M-2. This eastward freight at Lilly, Pennsylvania, on June 23, 2006, demonstrates the difference in radiator profiles between the leading SD70M and the trailing SD70M-2. *Brian Solomon*

Union Pacific No. 3934 is a long way from home rails on October 17, 2008, as it leads an eastward CSX freight on the former New York Central Water Level Route at Upton Road in Batavia, New York. UP bought large numbers of SD70Ms in the early 2000s. Today this model remains the most common locomotive on the railroad. *Brian Solomon*

This view of a westward UP freight at James, California, offers an excellent comparison of the different radiator profiles of three modern EMD locomotives. In the lead is an SD90/43MAC with the large radiator designed for EMD's 265H engine (although the locomotive is powered by a 16-710G3B). It is followed by one of UP's late-era SD70Ms with gently angled radiator intakes and an early-era SD70M with a conventional radiator profile. Increasingly stringent EPA emissions requirements have been met, in part, by increasing radiator capacity. *Brian Solomon*

In 1999, Union Pacific ordered 1,000 "retro" SD70Ms. Instead of modern desktop electronics, these featured conventional analog engineer controls and other low-tech equipment, such as mechanical fuel injection in place of electronic fuel injection. On Halloween Day 2003, UP No. 4209 was working toward Donner Summit with a westbound freight when it crawled past Old Gorge east of Alta, California. Lost in the fog is the American River, some 2,000 feet lower than rail level. *Brian Solomon*

On June 24, 1996, Canadian National SD70I No. 5603 winds through Steward, Illinois, westbound on BNSF's former Chicago, Burlington & Quincy line between Chicago and the Twin Cities. In the mid-1990s CN ordered a fleet of 4,000-horsepower SD70Is followed by 4,300-horsepower SD75Is. Both featured EMD's isolated whisper cab. Because output was adjusted with software changes, there were no differentiating external features between the two models, except for slight changes to the paint schemes. *Brian Solomon*

CN SD75I No. 5788 works west on the main line at Coteau, Quebec, on October 23, 2004. One way to quickly spot the difference between CN's SD70I and SD75I (as built) is the larger CN logo on the SD75Is, which extends above the handrails. *Brian Solomon*

For a few years in the mid-1990s, CN routed traffic between Duluth, Minnesota, and Chicago over Burlington Northern (BNSF after 1995) routes. Later, CN shifted its traffic to a Wisconsin Central routing in a prelude to CN's acquisition of that line. In July 1996, an eastward CN freight rolls toward Steward, Illinois, with a relatively new SD70I. *Brian Solomon*

New BNSF SD75Ms work west of Craig, Kansas, in February 1996. EMD's SD75M was a variation of the SD70M that uses the same hardware but uses software to deliver 4,300 horsepower instead of 4,000. These two extra-clean locomotives arrived the previous night on an executive business car special from Phoenix, Arizona. *Chris Guss*

This SD75M was the very last new locomotive delivered to Santa Fe Railway before its amalgamation into BNSF in September 1995. *Brian Solomon*

In 1995, Santa Fe ordered SD75Ms for Super Fleet intermodal services, such as No. 207, photographed at Corwith Yard, Chicago, on July 2, 1995. New SD75Ms early in the BNSF era were dressed in Santa Fe's war bonnet paint with BNSF lettering on the sides and "Santa Fe" in the front herald. *Brian Solomon*

Burlington Northern was first to order EMD's pioneering commercial heavy-haul, three-phase AC-traction diesel. Although BN/BNSF acquired SD70MACs specifically for Power River Basin coal traffic, AC-traction diesel-electric locomotives occasionally wander from the coal pool to other services. In October 2002, a pair of BNSF SD70MACs leads a CSX freight past vintage General Railway Signal semaphores on the former Monon at Romney, Indiana. *Brian Solomon*

Above: BNSF SD70MACs lead a Powder River Coal train on September 13, 2008. Key to the SD70MAC design is a pair of high-voltage inverters that convert DC power to modulated AC used for traction. Railroads are keen to use AC-traction locomotives in heavy service because modern AC motors allow for significantly greater tractive effort while requiring less maintenance and are not at risk from overloading. *Philip A. Brahms*

Opposite bottom: In the fading light of February 1997, a trio of BNSF SD70MACs in their as-delivered Grinstein Green (so named for BN chairman Gerald Grinstein) and cream paint work a loaded coal train toward Colorado's Palmer Divide. The ability of three AC-traction SD70MACs to replace five traditional 3,000-horsepower DC-traction diesels in coal service offered BN a substantial cost savings that encouraged the railroad to place a significant order for the new type. Although AC technology was not a new concept, EMD needed to adapt European AC-traction systems to the rigors of American freight railroading. *Brian Solomon*

New CSX SD70MACs leading a loaded coal train eastward meet SD50 No. 8552 working west at Cumberland, Maryland, on September 25, 1997. Locomotive No. 712 was from the first of several CSX orders for SD70MACs. CSX assigned its first SD70MACs to coal service on former Baltimore & Ohio lines, while later locomotives were bought for more varied duties around the system. *Brian Solomon*

On April 6, 2004, new CSX SD70MAC No. 4765 and an AC6000CW leading an eastward freight have just passed Washington Summit in the Berkshires of western Massachusetts. CSX's later SD70MACs featured tapered radiators with a greater cooling surface necessary to comply with more stringent emissions requirements. *Brian Solomon*

A pair of SD70MACs working west with an empty autorack train Q283 ascend the former Boston & Albany grade over Washington Hill near milepost 129 on October 5, 2007. CSX No. 4709 lacks its identifying nose herald. *Brian Solomon*

Above: Kansas City Southern No. 3905 leads train IJALZ-28 (Intermodal–Jackson, Mississippi, to Lazaro Cardenas, Mexico) north of Lucas, Louisiana, on April 28, 2008. To better align the motive power needs of the new KCS system, former TFM SD70MACs were reassigned to the KCS property in the United States while the KCS SD60s were sent to Mexico. The AC-traction locomotives are better suited for graded territory south of Kansas City. *Chris Guss*

Opposite top: TFM No. 1602 is part of a distributed power consist on the rear of a KCS coal empty just south of Anderson, Missouri. Over the years, KCS has tried manned helpers and remote-controlled consists over its two major grades, but AC-traction locomotives and distributed power have become KCS's new standard for moving tonnage on this busy Midwest corridor. *Chris Guss*

Opposite bottom: KCS No. 3920 started life as TFM No. 1620, but now wears its new reporting marks as it undergoes an overhaul at KCS' Shreveport, Louisiana, shops. It and the other 74 TFM SD70MACs will receive the same treatment as they begin their second life hauling tonnage in the Midwest after a decade of service in Mexico. TFM was one of six railroads that ordered the SD70MAC over the model's 11-year production span. *Chris Guss*

Only Conrail bought the SD80MAC, and it acquired 30 of the 5,000-horsepower model in the mid-1990s. Powered by a 20-cylinder 710G3 diesel, these big locomotives were the railroad's first AC-traction locomotives and briefly held the title as America's most powerful single-engine, single-unit diesel electrics. On August 30, 1997, a pair of SD80MACs and a pair of GE B23-7s work east of Hinsdale, Massachusetts, near Washington Summit with a heavy eastward freight.
Brian Solomon

New Conrail SD80MAC No. 4104 leads an eastward freight past the Twin Ledges east of Becket, Massachusetts, in October 1996. In Conrail's final years, it routinely assigned pairs of SD80MACs to Boston Line freights. When CSX assumed operations of this route in 1999, the 20-cylinder EMDs were largely reassigned to other duties. *Brian Solomon*

The SD80MAC measured 80 feet 2 inches long, weighed approximately 430,000 pounds fully serviceable, and could deliver 185,000 pounds starting tractive effort. When CSX and Norfolk Southern divided Conrail in 1999, each inherited some of the unique SD80MAC fleet. NS has primarily assigned its locomotives to coal service out of South Fork, Pennsylvania. On June 24, 2006, NS No. 7203 works a coal train at Summerhill, Pennsylvania. *Brian Solomon*

EMD's 6,000-horsepower locomotive was delayed while it refined its 265H engine. In the interim, it offered the "upgradeable" SD9043MAC, delivered with the older 16-710G3B engine rated at 4,300 horsepower. CP Rail No. 9125 leads an eastward intermodal at Boston Bar, British Columbia, on August 10, 1999. Due to costs and logistical issues, none of the convertible locomotives were ever upgraded. *Chris Guss*

Above: To achieve 6,000 horsepower with a single-engine locomotive, EMD introduced its four-cycle 265H engine—model GM16V265—to power the SD90MAC-H. In practice these locomotives were less common than the similar-looking SD9043MAC upgradeable types. Union Pacific SD90MAC-H No. 8535 was at Chicago's Clearing Yard diesel shop on June 30, 2000. *Chris Guss*

Opposite bottom: To avoid confusion between the 4,300-horsepower variation and the true 6,000-horsepower locomotive, various designations have been used for the "upgradeables," including SD9043MAC, SD90/43MAC, and SD9043AC. Both CP Rail and Union Pacific ordered upgradeable and new 6,000-horsepower variations. In July 2005, near Troy, California, a GE leads a pair of UP SD9043ACs working east toward Donner Summit. *Brian Solomon*

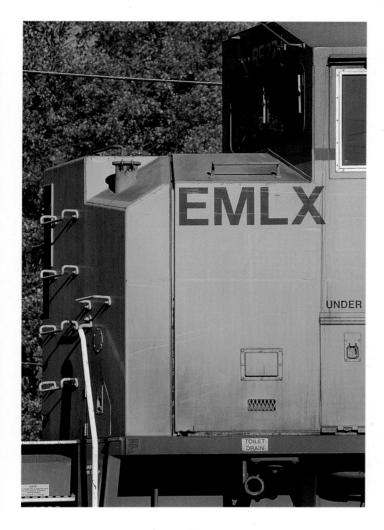

EMD's modern cab was introduced during production of UP's SD90MAC-H. While some of the locomotives featured the new cab, others featured the older style of North American Safety Cab introduced in the early 1990s for use on the SD60 and applied to the SD9043AC "upgradeables." Today, the modern angular cab style is standard on both the SD70M-2 and SD70ACe. *Brian Solomon*

Opposite top: Genesee & Wyoming short line Buffalo & Pittsburgh was among the last railroads to operate SD90MAC-Hs in heavy freight service. A pair of former Union Pacific SD90MAC-Hs leased by EMLX leads B&P's southward freight at East Salamanca, New York, on October 18, 2008. *Brian Solomon*

Opposite bottom: Former UP No. 8527 leads a B&P freight on October 11, 2008. The 6,000-horsepower SD90MAC-H was among the most interesting, although unsuccessful, modern diesels. Compared with other models, the majority of SD90MAC-Hs had very short service lives—the unusual engine and reported lower-than-anticipated availability, combined with the nonstandard horsepower rating, contributed to their early retirement. Most of the big units have been scrapped. *Brian Solomon*

Above: On August 14, 2009, a westward Union Pacific double-stack passes the siding at Elsie, Oregon, on the former Western Pacific. This broadside image offers a good comparison between the SD70ACe (leading) and an upgradeable SD9043AC. The SD70ACe is just 74 feet 3 inches long, compared to 80 feet 2 inches. Both locomotives have AC traction and are rated at 4,300 horsepower, but the ACe is a more modern design built to comply with the more stringent EPA Tier 2 emissions requirements. *Brian Solomon*

Opposite top: UP SD70ACe No. 8341 rolls east through Colfax, California, with a train ascending toward Donner Pass. Since 2005, the SD70ACe has been EMD's standard AC-traction freight locomotive. The small letter "e" in the designation stands for "enhanced," reflecting changes to the engine design. *Brian Solomon*

Opposite bottom: On May 6, 2010, UP SD70ACe No. 1995 leads the company business train near Canal Street in Chicago. This is one of several locomotives dressed in special heritage liveries resembling paint schemes used by railroads absorbed by Union Pacific. UP melded the old Chicago & North Western into its system in 1995. *Chris Guss*

CSX SD70ACe No. 4834 and an SD70MAC drift downgrade with an eastward freight on the old Boston & Albany main line east of Middlefield, Massachusetts, on May 4, 2007. EMD specifications indicate an SD70ACe offers 106,000 pounds braking effort, compared with just 86,850 pounds on the SD70M-2. Externally the two locomotives look almost identical—the primary difference is their AC and DC traction systems. *Brian Solomon*

In October 2005, a nearly new CSX SD70ACe leads an eastward freight by the former Boston & Albany passenger station at Warren, Massachusetts. Seventy-nine years earlier, New York Central's B&A invested in extremely powerful Lima 2-8-4 steam locomotives, named Berkshires in honor of the line. Where a Class A1a 2-8-4 offered 81,400 pounds tractive effort with a booster, today's SD70ACe can deliver 191,000 pounds. *Brian Solomon*

CSX SD70ACe No. 4809 works singly with a southward freight past the Richmond, Virginia, Amtrak station on the former Richmond, Fredericksburg & Potomac in early October 2005. *Brian Solomon*

Three-phase AC traction made its debut in Powder River coal service on BNSF predecessor Burlington Northern. Today, BNSF continues to buy the most modern AC-traction diesels for this same service. On September 27, 2009, BNSF SD70ACe No. 9355 leads a loaded unit train on the Orin Line south of Gillette, Wyoming. *Patrick Yough*

BNSF SD70ACe No. 9206 catches the afternoon sun under a big sky on September 28, 2009. The advent of distributed power technology has changed the way BNSF assigns locomotives to heavy trains. Where in 1994, three SD70MACs would have led a loaded unit coal train, today it is typical for two modern ACs to lead and one to work as a radio-controlled DPU at the back of the train. BNSF operates approximately 80 percent of its unit coal trains with DPUs. *Patrick Yough*

BNSF SD70ACe No. 9230 shows off its fresh paint. *Patrick Yough*

Kansas City Southern SD70ACe No. 4115 leads a unit grain extra north of Rich Mountain, Arkansas, on April 27, 2008. *Chris Guss*

In the early 2000s, KCS began ordering freight diesels in a paint scheme that was a close adaptation of its 1940s-era streamliner, *Southern Belle*. On April 29, 2008, SD70ACe No. 4108 and a new General Electric ES44AC lead a unit grain train at DeQuincy, Louisiana. *Chris Guss*

As spring foliage begins to emerge, KCS SD70ACe No. 4013 leads an intermodal train north of Hatton, Arkansas. Rated at 4,300 horsepower, a single SD70ACe has sufficient power to move a relatively light train. *Chris Guss*

On June 13, 2008, a new pair of Montana Rail Link SD70ACe diesels lead westward freight LM (Laurel to Missoula) out of the west portal of the summit tunnel on Mullen Pass. This former Northern Pacific crossing of the Continental Divide is operated by MRL today but still carries a considerable volume of BNSF through freight. *Tom Kline*

MRL SD70Ace locomotives are head-end helpers leading a westward BNSF loaded coal train on the Austin Creek Trestle at Austin, Montana, toward the summit of the Continental Divide. Until its acquisition of 16 SD70ACe locomotives in 2005, MRL operated its entire railroad with second-hand diesels, including a substantial fleet of EMDs powered by the 1960s-era 20-645E3 engine rated at 3,600 horsepower. *Tom Kline*

In the final twinkle of sun on the western side of the Continental Divide, Montana Rail Link SD70ACe No. 4301 rolls downgrade with the Laurel-to-Missoula symbol freight LM. MRL's 16 SD70ACe locomotives are numbered 4300–4315. *Tom Kline*

New Norfolk Southern SD70M-2 No. 2667 works westward and catches the attention of visitors at Pennsylvania's famous Horseshoe Curve on June 23, 2006. Today this modern diesel does the job once performed by Pennsylvania Railroad's massive steam locomotives. *Brian Solomon*

NS SD70M-2 No. 2735 leads eastward intermodal train No. 168 on Canadian Pacific's Delaware & Hudson route near Worcester, New York, on October 10, 2007. NS has opted to purchase EMD's DC-traction diesels rather than the more expensive AC-traction models. *Brian Solomon*

Canadian National has not embraced the AC-traction trend. Instead it has purchased DC-traction models exclusively from both General Electric and EMD in recent years. On September 9, 2009, SD70M-2 No. 8805 leads train 406 at Rothesay, New Brunswick.
George S. Pitarys

Passenger Locomotives

While passenger locomotives are highly specialized designs representing only a small portion of locomotives manufactured, people tend to be more familiar with these locomotives than the hoards of heavy-haul freight diesels. Where the 410 SD9043MACs in freight service seem relatively unusual to the casual observer, the 207 P42DC Genesis locomotives built for Amtrak are emblematic of contemporary U.S. intercity passenger operations.

Compared with freight diesels, where a few standard types ordered in large numbers to nearly identical specifications satisfy the bulk of the market, passenger locomotives tend to be tailored to individual buyer specifications and purchased in small batches. Complicating the passenger locomotive business is the fact that most essential North American locomotive technologies have been developed and refined for the demands of the more lucrative freight locomotive business. The result is that locomotive technology must be adapted at relatively high cost to the specific services demanded by passenger applications. In the 1960s, 1970s, and 1980s, passenger locomotives were derived

from freight models, with only very slight changes, such as the addition of head-end electrical power for heating and lighting trains. Since the 1990s, while primary components for passenger locomotives have been essentially the same as those for freight diesels, locomotive configuration has blended American and European technologies in an effort to produce machines better suited to passenger services.

Traditionally, passenger locomotives have been built by the same firms that focus on freight locomotives; since the 1960s this has largely been EMD and GE. During the 1980s and 1990s, remanufactured locomotives for passenger applications were developed by several smaller manufacturers, such as MotivePower's predecessor, MK Rail. Since 2000, changes in the locomotive marketplace, predicated by ever stricter environmental controls, have resulted in the commercial obsolescence of EMD's and GE's established passenger types, leaving the market open to smaller builders.

When Amtrak sought to replace its fleet of aging 1970s-era Electro-Motive F40PHs in the 1990s, it was unwilling to settle for adaptations of existing freight locomotives.

Among the most interesting diesels in North America are NJ Transit's 33 PL42-ACs built by Alstom at the former Erie Railroad shops in Hornell, New York. These are a unique melding of European and North American technologies unlike anything operating on either continent. They are powered by an EMD 16-710G3B-T1 diesel and rated at 4,200 horsepower. Atypical of North American diesels is their unusual European-style traction system. *Patrick Yough*

GE and EMD placed bids for a modern, lightweight, state-of-the-art locomotive, with GE winning the contract. GE worked with Amtrak in the design, incorporating several European concepts. GE designated the resulting type as its Genesis line. Among the distinct characteristics of the Genesis are fabricated trucks in place of conventional cast-steel trucks and a monocoque body shell that's integral with the locomotive structure, rather than a nonstructural covering atop a platform.

GE developed three Genesis models. The first was the 4,000-horsepower Dash 8-40BP (sometimes known as the P40), of which 44 were built for Amtrak numbered in

Previous pages:
Amtrak F59PHI with a *Pacific Surfliner* at San Diego in June 2008 represents modern passenger locomotives used on the West Coast. These 3,200-horsepower streamlined diesels are well suited to medium-distance passenger runs where rapid acceleration is desirable. *Brian Solomon*

the 800 series. Later GE refined its design, producing the 4,200-horsepower P42DC built for both Amtrak and Canadian intercity passenger provider VIA Rail. A significantly different dual-mode variety, the P32AC-DM was designed for service on New York–area third-rail DC-electrified lines. Able to operate as both as a diesel-electric and as a straight electric in third-rail territory, this model also employs an alternating current (AC) traction system, rather than the more conventional direct current (DC) traction used on most passenger locomotives.

In the mid-1980s, EMD designed its F59PH model for short-haul passenger services. This wide-nose cab type used EMD's state-of-the-art 710 series engine and modern electrics refined for its 60-series freight diesels. Initially these models were sold to Toronto-based Government of Ontario (GO) Transit, and later to Los Angeles Metrolink.

In the 1990s, EMD adapted the technology used in the F59PH for a new locomotive that complied with California's strict air-quality requirements and had a modern crash-resistant streamlined body featuring the whisper cab. Designated the F59PHI, this 3,200-horsepower model has been ordered for Amtrak corridor services on the West Coast, as well as by the North Carolina Department of Transportation for Amtrak services and by a variety of commuter railroads. EMD also sold specialized 3,000-horsepower models to New York's Long Island Rail Road: One model was a conventional diesel-electric passenger locomotive in a low-clearance body, the other was a very similar-appearing dual-mode type for third-rail service into Penn Station.

Increasingly stringent demands on emissions, combined with new crash-worthiness standards, have made the comparatively small market for passenger locomotives uneconomic to the large locomotive manufacturers. Today, passenger diesels often cost twice that of new freight power. Instead of engineering and building very small fleets of custom-designed passenger locomotives, EMD and GE have acted as suppliers, providing primary components to smaller manufacturers.

MotivePower's MPXpress models have been the most common types purchased by North American commuter railroads in the last decade. Three models have been offered that use EMD-designed engines, trucks, and traction motors in a futuristic-looking locomotive body. In addition, Alstom has built an unusual-looking high-horsepower passenger diesel for New Jersey–based NJ Transit, while Pennsylvania-based Brookville has constructed road switcher–style locomotives for Metro-North and the Connecticut Department of Transportation.

Opposite: One of the United States' newest commuter train services is the *North Star*, which began operations from Minneapolis to far-flung northwestern exurbs in November 2009. The trains serve the downtown Target Field terminal just around the corner from the Voyageur Press offices. The *North Star* operates with five MotivePower MP36PH-3Cs. *Brian Solomon*

In June 2008, a Metrolink F59PHI leads an outbound train at Burbank. The F59PHI was EMD's standard passenger locomotive introduced in the mid-1990s. The model shares styling queues with automotive minivans built by parent company General Motors at about the same time. The model became one of the most common for West Coast services, which expanded rapidly during the 1990s. *Brian Solomon*

On June 30, 2010, Amtrak train No. 42, *The Pennsylvanian*, works east on the former Pennsylvania Railroad main line at Summerhill, Pennsylvania. GE Genesis model P42 No. 44 has the historical significance of having led President Barack Obama's inauguration special on January 17, 2009. Genesis models compose the bulk of Amtrak's intercity diesel locomotive fleet. *Brian Solomon*

New Mexico's Rail Runner suburban service began operations in 2006. Today, its route connects the cities of Santa Fe, Albuquerque, and Belen. By mid-2010, Rail Runner was one of eight North American commuter railways to receive MotivePower's MP36PH-3C diesel-electric locomotives. On St. Patrick's Day 2009, Rail Runner No. 106 passes a former Union Switch & Signal Style-T upper-quadrant semaphore near Bernalillo, New Mexico. *Tim Doherty*

Amtrak General Electric Dash 8-32BWH No. 502 with a *Capitols* train is seen at 16th Street Station in Oakland, California, in 1992. Amtrak's 20 Dash 8-32BWHs built in 1991 were similar to Santa Fe Railway's Dash 8-40BWs freight locomotives and share most external dimensions. However, Amtrak's Dash 8-32BWH is powered by a 12-cylinder FDL engine rated at 3,200 horsepower for traction. An extra alternator is used to produce head-end power for passenger cars—thus the *H* in the locomotive designation. *Brian Solomon*

No. 502 leads a Sacramento-to-San Jose *Capitols* service along the shore of San Pablo Bay near Pinole, California. The new Amtrak livery on these GEs earned the Dash 8-32BWHs the nickname "Pepsi cans." Locomotive Nos. 501 and 502 were funded by the California Department of Transportation, thus indicated by the small blue CT on the nose of the locomotive. *Brian Solomon*

Amtrak's "Pepsi can" scheme was short-lived. On November 12, 2003, Amtrak No. 505, wearing a minimalist Platinum Mist livery, leads a *San Joaquin* train from Bakersfield, California, through Oakland's Jack London Square. Amtrak's order for Dash 8-32BWHs was a prelude to the development of the streamlined Genesis type introduced in 1993. *Brian Solomon*

Amtrak P42DC No. 63, in its as-delivered paint, leads the eastward *Pennsylvanian* near Cresson, Pennsylvania, on the former Pennsylvania Railroad main line. The P42DC was the most common model of General Electric's Genesis. The 4,250-horsepower locomotive began production in 1996 and was sold to both Amtrak and VIA Rail for long-distance passenger services. As built, the P42DC complied with EPA Tier 0 emissions standards. *Brian Solomon*

In October 2000, Amtrak P42DC No. 1, dressed in the Northeast Direct scheme, speeds train No. 449— the westward Boston section of the *Lake Shore Limited*—over the Quaboag River near West Warren, Massachusetts. This Genesis series is no longer produced, in part, because the design complies with neither current EPA emissions standards nor contemporary crashworthiness requirements. *Brian Solomon*

An unusual route for an Amtrak Genesis locomotive is the old Rutland Railroad line via Mount Holly, Vermont. While not part of a regular Amtrak service, on October 4, 2004, a pair of P42DCs leads the *American Orient Express*, a high-priced tour train using 1940s and 1950s streamlined equipment. The train is crossing Vermont Rail System's high trestle at Cuttingsville on its way to Bellows Falls, Vermont. *Brian Solomon*

General Electric's P32AC-DM is a specialized dual-mode (hence "DM") machine that can operate using electricity from New York City–area third rail as well as diesel power. It succeeded EMD's FL9, a type designed in the 1950s for the New Haven Railroad and that worked for many years in New York suburban services. On June 27, 1997, a new Amtrak P32AC-DM leads an Empire Corridor train north in the Hudson Valley toward Albany. *Brian Solomon*

Metro-North operates a fleet of P32AC-DMs on its push-pull suburban services to Grand Central Station. In electrified territory these locomotives can draw current from the line-side third rail, although in routine operations they tend to run as diesels until reaching the Park Avenue Tunnel. On July 9, 2004, at Scarborough, New York, on the former New York Central Hudson Division, No. 227 shoves its train toward New York City. *Brian Solomon*

The Connecticut Department of Transportation purchased four of the P32AC-DMs operated by Metro-North. These are painted in a modern adaptation of New Haven Railroad's famous McGinnis livery best remembered as the scheme used on the dual-mode FL9s. This view of P32AC-DM No. 229 in May 2007 was taken on the former New Haven Railroad at Danbury. *Brian Solomon*

In 2001, Canada's intercity passenger service operator, VIA Rail, acquired a fleet of 20 Genesis P42DCs from General Electric. VIA Rail No. 908 crosses the Lachine Canal in Montreal in October 2004. *Brian Solomon*

VIA Rail typically assigns its Genesis diesels to 1980s-era LRC trains working in the Quebec City–Montreal–Ottawa–Toronto–Windsor corridor. LRC stands for "Light, Rapid, Comfortable" and uses passenger cars with a tilting design built by Bombardier. Originally these trains were hauled by futuristic-looking LRC diesels powered by the Alco-designed 251 engine. *Brian Solomon*

On October 10, 2009, two VIA Rail P42DCs work west at Spadina Avenue after departing Toronto Union Station. *Brian Solomon*

Right: A Chicago Metra F40PHM-2 works west across the diamonds at Joliet, Illinois, on July 30, 1994. This model was unique to the commuter rail operator. Internally, it was very similar to the F40PH-2 and shared its 3,000 horsepower rating; externally, it featured a distinctive cab profile reaching to the front of the locomotive and lacking the distinct nose section featured on F40 models. *Brian Solomon*

Below: EMD developed the F40PH-2 for Amtrak in the mid-1970s and the model remained as a standard new passenger type through the 1980s. In 1990 Metra ordered this variation of the type designated F40PHM-2. Metra's former Burlington commuter route to Aurora serves La Grange, Illinois, pictured here on July 4, 2005. Ironically EMD's La Grange plant ended regular locomotive assembly following completion of the last Metra F40PHM-2 in December 1992. *Brian Solomon*

Opposite: Metra's F40PHM-2s were known colloquially as Winnebagos because of their resemblance to the popular brand of motor home. On June 22, 2004, Metra No. 201 departs Union Station in Chicago with an Aurora-bound suburban train. *Brian Solomon*

Above: Government of Ontario, which operates an intensive suburban service radiating from Toronto Union Station, worked with EMD in the design of a suitable commuter locomotive. A GO Transit F59PH races toward Toronto Union Station on February 8, 2010. Powered by a 12-cylinder 710G3 diesel, the F59PH shares most of its mechanical and electrical equipment with the streamlined F59PHI. *Brian Solomon*

Opposite: For two decades, EMD F59PHs working in push-pull service have provided most of GO Transit's motive power needs. During 2009 and 2010, GO bought new MP40s from MotivePower to supplant the aging F59PHs. *Brian Solomon*

Los Angeles Metrolink developed a commuter rail system for Southern California that was closely modeled on GO Transit's successful strategy. Metrolink bought a small fleet of F59PHs, making it the only other buyer of this relatively unusual model. Between runs, Metrolink No. 860 lays over at Oceanside, California, on May 31, 2008. *Brian Solomon*

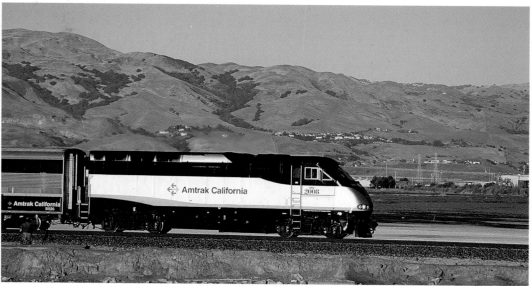

Above: EMD adapted its existing F59PH suburban rail-service locomotive into the F59PHI—a powerful, streamlined diesel-electric that complied with strict California emission requirements. On November 4, 2003, F59PHI No. 2012, lettered for Amtrak California, leads a *Capitols* service arriving at San Jose. The F59PHI's bulbous nose is a fiberglass composite; thick steel plates beneath it help protect the crew. This design is safer than the 1940s-era streamlined "bulldog" nose used on EMD E- and F-units. Brian *Solomon*

Opposite top: Amtrak F59PHI No. 450 works at the back of a *Pacific Surfliner* passing Del Mar, California. While General Electric's Genesis models have become standard for most Amtrak long-distance services, EMD's F59PHI is the most common type on various West Coast corridor trains. *Brian Solomon*

Opposite bottom: The modern-looking F59PHI was styled to match specially designed bi-level low-entry "California cars." On September 15, 2009, Amtrak No. 2008 crosses wetlands at Alviso, California, with a *Capitols* train. *Brian Solomon*

The North Carolina DOT bought two F59PHIs in 1998 for use on the *Piedmont. City of Salisbury* and *City of Asheville* carry road numbers that represent the founding dates of those cities and represent an operational anomaly: The majority of F59PHIs in the United States are assigned to West Coast passenger services. *Brian Solomon*

Amtrak's Raleigh-to-Charlotte *Piedmont* approaches its station stop at Durham, North Carolina, on February 19, 2004. This three-car train is hauled by F59PHI No. 1755, *City of Salisbury*. The North Carolina Department of Transportation funds the train and, because of lower long-term operating costs, made the unusual choice of buying new EMD locomotives to haul refurbished heritage passenger equipment. *Brian Solomon*

Montreal commuter train operator Agence métropolitaine de transport (AMT) operates 11 EMD F59PHIs (Nos. 1320–1330) built in 2000 and 2001. On August 16, 2004, No. 1325 is seen at Vendome Station across from a rebuilt GP9, classed GP9RM. AMT's F59PHIs primarily work the CP Rail route between Montreal and Vaudreuil-Hudson, Quebec (a commuter route that formerly ended at Dorion). *Tim Doherty*

Above: Long Island Rail Road's EMD DM30AC was designed specifically for New York–area suburban service. It features 45-inch wheels and a 92:19 gear ratio with Siemens-designed AC traction motors capable of 100-mile-per-hour service. *Brian Solomon*

Opposite bottom: LIRR's dual-mode DM30AC No. 500 leads a train of bi-level Kawasaki cars on the Central Branch at Bethpage, New York, on April 20, 2000. LIRR operates one of the most intensive commuter rail networks in the United States. These modern EMD passenger locomotives are unique to LIRR and are custom-designed with a low profile to accommodate tight clearances in the New York City area. *Patrick Yough*

On March 12, 2003, LIRR DM30AC No. 510 approaches Jamaica, Queens, with a double-deck suburban train. LIRR's 23 DM30ACs (sometimes classified as DE30AC-DMs) are modern dual-mode locomotives rated at 3,000-horsepower. They can operate as normal diesel-electric locomotives or draw current from a high-voltage DC third rail. Numbered in the 500 series, they are similar in appearance to LIRR's 23 400 series DE30ACs, which are diesel-electric only.
Brian Solomon

Above: Brookville's BL20GH rides on Blomberg trucks powered by D78 traction motors. On July 20, 2010, a Connecticut Department of Transportation Brookville-built BL20GH leads an afternoon train from Waterbury along the electrified former New Haven Railroad main line. *Patrick Yough*

Opposite top: On June 9, 2008—its first day of public operation—CDOT Brookville-built BL20GH No. 125 leads train No. 1906 at Waterbury. CDOT bought six of these unusual locomotives, primarily to replace its aging FL9s and FP10s on branch passenger trains. *Otto M. Vondrak*

Opposite bottom: Dressed in a livery inspired by the New Haven Railroad's famous McGinnis paint scheme, BL20GH No. 125 leads train No. 1841 at Stamford on July 6, 2009. *Otto M. Vondrak*

In 2003, Caltrain Peninsula service, which operates the former Southern Pacific commutes between San Francisco and San Jose (and a few trains to Gilroy), was the first to acquire MotivePower's MPXpress commuter locomotives. These were bought for service expansion and improvement in the form of the "Baby Bullet" limited express trains designed to cut running time between main terminals and provide additional services at rush hours. The locomotives arrived prior to introduction of Baby Bullet services and initially worked ordinary Caltrain runs. *Brian Solomon*

Caltrain MP36PH-3C No. 927 departs Millbrae Station on August 13, 2009, with a San Jose–bound Baby Bullet. These 3,600-horsepower locomotives have 20 percent more horsepower than Caltrain's 1980s-era EMD F40PH-2s. *Brian Solomon*

A San Francisco–bound Baby Bullet roars past California Avenue Station in Palo Alto. Today these powerful diesels roar over the line once famous for Southern Pacific's *Daylight* streamliners. *Brian Solomon*

An MP36PH-3S and an F40PHM-2 work a westward "scoot" running from Chicago Union Station to Aurora, Illinois, on the old Burlington route. As of late 2010, Chicago Metra has been the only operator of the MP36PH-3S variation of MotivePower's MPXpress passenger locomotive. The MP36PH-3S uses a static inverter driven by the prime mover for head-end power (HEP). The MP36PH-3C model produces HEP with an auxiliary diesel and separate generator. *Brian Solomon*

Metra MP36PH-3S No. 424 shoves at the back of a suburban train working toward Chicago Union Station on June 22, 2004. *Brian Solomon*

MotivePower MP40PH-3Cs have replaced 1980s-era EMD F59PHs as the standard locomotive on most GO Transit trains. All trains are push-pull sets with the locomotive on the east end. On June 11, 2010, GO Transit No. 631 shoves a westward train at Bathurst Street in Toronto. *Brian Solomon*

Toronto offers one of the best integrated public transportation networks in North America. Using GO Transit and Toronto Transit Commission subways, streetcars, and buses, it is easy to travel virtually anywhere in the metropolitan area without a car. *Brian Solomon*

Freezing conditions prevailed on February 8, 2010, as a GO Transit MP40PH-3C worked eastward with a train inbound for Toronto Union Station. Among GO Transit's unusual features is that many trains work through Union Station to outlying suburban terminals rather than terminating downtown. *Brian Solomon*

Switchers

Historically, switchers were among the most common types of diesel locomotives; however, from the 1960s through the 1980s, their market declined rapidly. Due to the nature of their service, switchers tend to have longer lifespans than road power and therefore require less frequent replacement. Also, many railroads cascaded old road diesels into switching duties rather than buy new switchers. Finally, a shift from small carload shipments to point-to-point intermodal and single-commodity unit trains, as well as a general decline in passenger services and moves to fixed passenger consists, further obviated the need for switchers.

In the 1990s, the market for new switchers heated up again. Modern high-horsepower road locomotives, which tend to be equipped with North American Safety Cabs, are poorly suited for most switching duties. Also, innovative technologies have made modern switching locomotives more economical to operate than traditional models. However, because demand for switchers is still relatively small, this market doesn't interest General Electric and EMD, so smaller manufacturers have developed the modern switcher business, building all-new switchers, as well as rebuilding, remanufacturing, or otherwise adapting older types with state-of-the-art equipment.

In the early 1990s, MK Rail (antecedent to today's MotivePower Industries) developed an experimental low-horsepower, low-emissions switcher that burned liquefied natural gas. While LNG-fueled locomotives did not catch on, during the last decade, development and application of Genset (a compact engine-generator set) technology has been one of the most successful means of reducing fuel consumption and lowering emissions for new switching locomotives. Low-emissions diesel Gensets are used in multiple in place of conventional single large diesel engines. Where a large engine must run all the time, individual Gensets are switched on only as needed, resulting in more efficient fuel consumption and much lower emissions. Computer controls may rotate the use of Gensets to ensure relatively even wear and maintenance.

Several railroads have entered public-private partnerships in which public agencies provide funding assistance for railroads to replace traditional diesels with new Genset locomotives. California and Texas, where emissions requirements are the most stringent, have led the nation in Genset locomotive applications.

In 2010, several manufacturers offered Genset locomotives, including National Railway Equipment, Railpower, Brookville, and MotivePower. NRE offers four Genset locomotive models in its N-ViroMotive line, including three four-axle, four-motor types: the 1GS-7B is a single-Genset locomotive rated at 700 horsepower; the 2GS-14B is a twin-Genset 1,400-horsepower model; and the 3GS-21B is a 2,100-horsepower triple-Genset aimed at replacing the 2,000 GP38s and GP38-2s in equivalent services. NRE's 3GS-21C, a triple-Genset six-motor model also rated at 2,100 horsepower, is roughly equivalent to an EMD SD38 and is intended for slow-speed, high tractive–effort applications, such as hump yard service. Most NRE locomotives use Cummins QSK19C diesels

Railpower, owned by short-line operator R. J. Corman since 2009, has enjoyed reasonable success with its range of Genset locomotives. These include two four-axle, four-motor models and one six-motor type.

The RP14BD is a twin-Genset type built on an old switcher platform and rated at 1,400 horsepower, while the RP20BD is a triple-Genset built on an old EMD GP9-era platform and rated at 2,000 horsepower. The six-motor RP20CD is built on an old EMD platform and rated at 2,000 horsepower. Typically, Railpower locomotives have employed Deutz V-8 diesels, although company literature notes that Cummins diesels are also available.

Union Pacific has been a leader in Genset locomotive development and application, and it has several fleets in dedicated service. As of August 2010, it rostered 175 units: a fleet of 60 NRE 2GS-21Bs (UP class 2GS-21B) and a lone 2GS-14B are assigned to California's Los Angeles Basin, while another fleet of 98 Railpower four-motor RP20Bs were based in Texas working largely around Ft. Worth and Houston. UP's smallest fleet consists of six-axle Railpower RP20CDs that work the former Southern Pacific yard at Roseville, California. BNSF also has a significant fleet of NRE and Railpower Gensets, largely assigned to terminals in California and Texas.

Previous pages:
Railpower RP20BD No. 5400 is a 2,000-horsepower switcher powered by three Deutz diesel Gensets (compact diesel-generator units). Although these modern switchers are commonly referred to as Gensets, the term properly applies to the powerplants within the locomotive, rather than the locomotive itself. *Pat Yough*

Because of ther low emissions, three-Genset, six-motor switching locomotives tend to be assigned in areas where pollution control has popular political considerations. *Brian Solomon*

Union Pacific No. 2690 is a Railpower three-Genset, four-motor RP20BD (also variously referred to as a RP20B and RP30GE) assigned to switching work in Texas. *Pat Yough*

UP has assigned six Railpower three-Genset, six-motor locomotives to the Roseville, California, hump yard. These are powered by Deutz diesels and designed for slow-speed high-tractive effort service. In May 2008, UP displayed one of the brand-new Genset locomotives at the California State Railroad Museum in Sacramento. *Brian Solomon*

Above: National Railway Equipment's four stock varieties of its N-ViroMotive Genset switchers were developed between 2001 and 2005 to meet strict air-quality regulations imposed by the California Air Quality Resources Board. BNSF 3GS-21B No. 1253, seen at Mykawa, Texas, on June 6, 2009, is a four-motor unit riding on Blomberg trucks with a 62:18 gear ratio and D77 traction motors. Its three 700-horsepower Gensets each use a Cummins QSK19 paired with a 572RDL generator. *Tom Kline*

Opposite top: California's Pacific Harbor Line acquired four National Railway Equipment four-motor 3GS-12B Genset locomotives during 2007 and 2008, and it also owns a pair of NRE's six-motor 3GS-12C Genset locomotives. The "B" and "C" designations denote four or six motors, as all axles are powered. Pacific Harbor Line provides switching at the ports of Los Angeles and Long Beach. *Brian Solomon*

Opposite bottom: BNSF switches at Point Richmond, California, with National Railway Equipment 3GS-12B Genset locomotive No. 1286 on May 29, 2010. *Philip A. Brahms*

547

A Buffalo & Pittsburgh crewman works Genesee & Wyoming locomotive No. 1401, a Brookville GS1400. This 1,400-horsepower locomotive features a pair of diesel Gensets, each using a Cummins QSK19 engine. The locomotive frame and some mechanical components have been recycled from an older EMD SW1500 switcher. Railroads can lower the emissions and improve the fuel economy of switching locomotives by replacing traditional large diesel engines with groups of two or more diesel Gensets because two (or more) Gensets are active only when the load on the locomotive requires greater power.
Patrick Yough

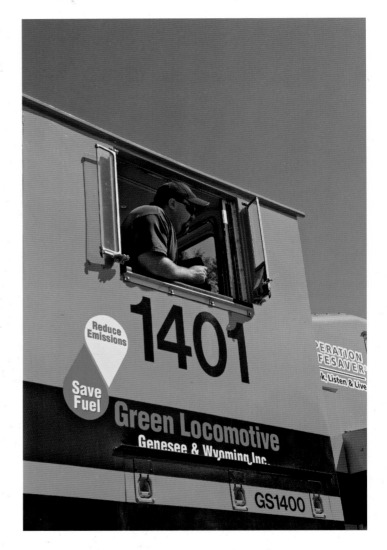

Brand-new G&W No. 1401 lettered for Buffalo & Pittsburgh works at Butler Yard near Punxsutawney, Pennsylvania, on July 17, 2010. G&W's Buffalo & Pittsburgh operates former Buffalo, Rochester & Pittsburgh trackage in western Pennsylvania and New York State acquired from CSX in 1988 as part of a regional spin-off. *Adam Stuebgen*

Two Port Terminal Railway Association MK1500Ds work a chemical train at Penn City Yard in Channelview, east of Houston, Texas, on June 12, 2004. MK Rail built 24 MK1500Ds in 1996 for the PTRA. These are the road's sole motive power for switching service in the Houston area. No. 9617 began its career as New York Central GP7 No. 5610 in the early 1950s. *Tom Kline*

BNSF MK1200G No. 1203 rests at San Pedro, California. Introduced in 1994 by MotivePower Industries predecessor MK Rail, this was an experimental low-emissions design powered by a Caterpillar G3516 engine and fueled by liquefied natural gas. Two were built for Santa Fe and two for Union Pacific. Today, BNSF rosters all four, which are usually assigned switching work in the Los Angeles area. *Brian Solomon*

This MK1500D was built at Boise, Idaho, in November 1996. After separating from MK Rail in 1996, MotivePower Industries was known as Boise Locomotive Company for three years until it merged with Westinghouse Air Brake Company. Today, MotivePower continues to build a variety of specialty locomotives. *Patrick Yough*

MotivePower built 13 MP20GPs for Union Pacific using old GP50 platforms. These are assigned to switching work in the Houston area. UP has numbered its switchers and other locomotives in yard work with UPY reporting marks. UPY No. 2109 was photographed at Houston, Texas, on April 1, 2007. *Tom Kline*

As traditional switchers wear out, the Class 1 railroads have had to replace them with new, rebuilt, or otherwise improved machines. *Tom Kline*

A detail view of a Union Pacific MP20GP control stand. *Tom Kline*

INDEX